GUIDANCE MONOGRAPH SERIES

SHELLEY C. STONE

BRUCE SHERTZER

Editors

GUIDANCE MONOGRAPH SERIES

The general purpose of Houghton Mifflin's Guidance Monograph Series is to provide high quality coverage of topics which are of abiding importance in contemporary counseling and guidance practice. In a rapidly expanding field of endeavor, change and innovation are inevitably present. A trend accompanying such growth is greater and greater specialization. Specialization results in an increased demand for materials which reflect current modifications in guidance practice while simultaneously treating the field in greater depth and detail than commonly found in textbooks and brief journal articles.

The list of eminent contributors to this series assures the reader expert treatment of the areas covered. The monographs are designed for consumers with varying familiarity to the counseling and guidance field. The editors believe that the series will be useful to experienced practitioners as well as beginning students. While these groups may use the monographs with somewhat different goals in mind, both will benefit from the treatment given to content areas.

The content areas treated have been selected because of specific criteria. Among them are timeliness, practicality, and persistency of the issues involved. Above all, the editors have attempted to select topics which are of major substantive concern to counseling and guidance personnel.

Shelley C. Stone

Bruce Shertzer

DECISION-MAKING

AND

VOCATIONAL

DEVELOPMENT

EDWIN L. HERR

THE PENNSYLVANIA STATE UNIVERSITY

HOUGHTON MIFFLIN COMPANY · BOSTON

NEW YORK · ATLANTA · GENEVA, ILL. · DALLAS · PALO ALTO

DEDICATION

To Amber Leigh and Christopher Alan
For many meaningful and productive tomorrows

ACKNOWLEDGMENTS

To my respected colleague, George Hudson, and to my student and friend, Edward Smith, my appreciation for their critical review and comments about the separate chapters. The resulting weaknesses of the manuscript reflect the limitations of the author, not the insights of these reviewers.

To Mrs. Patricia Tate for her patient and dedicated typing of the manuscript, my appreciation and thanks.

To my wife, Pat, for her enduring support and encouragement, my love.

E. L. H.

The Pennsylvania State University

CONTENTS

EDITORS' INTRODUCTION

This monograph is devoted to a consideration of decision-making and vocational development. These are important matters for counselors. Unfortunately, they are processes that are not as well understood as they should be because they are intricate, interacting and subtle. Despite these difficulties, the fact remains that one of the hardest tasks a counselor faces is to discover ways in which he can facilitate and advance these complex processes among those he serves. It is quite certain that there is no easy or magical solution for him to call upon.

Decision-making and vocational development are phenomena of human experience and in that sense, therefore, they are *meaningful*. But to explain either of them, the observer must understand not only how various factors combine, but how they interrelate, the manner in which respective modes enter into the causal process, and the like. Edwin Herr, the author of this monograph, has sought to describe and clarify these processes. He defines vocational development and decision-making, presents a brief overview of theory building in the area and the factors involved in it and suggests some guidance strategies designed to facilitate these processes with elementary and secondary school students. Dr. Herr has incorporated and condensed a vast amount of material pertinent to his explication of decision-making and vocational development. He has carefully limited his discussion to informative and crucial areas.

We believe that students of guidance and practitioners will find this monograph useful in understanding decision-making and vocational development. The author's description of guidance strategies (Chapter Five) contains many suggestions which, if implemented, would be of direct benefit to students.

SHELLEY C. STONE

BRUCE SHERTZER

AUTHOR'S INTRODUCTION

The range of human behavior to which school counselors must respond, which they must develop or assist their counselees to redirect is vast indeed. As the implications of individual differences and understandings of the influences which shape such differences have continued to surface, guidance strategies and emphases have shifted and the professional maturity of guidance practitioners has accelerated. In consequence, the conceptual structures and the practices which have shaped public school guidance programs continue to be refined as a heritage of insights from many disciplines is synthesized and systematized.

In few other areas is the base of knowledge about human behavior expanding more purposefully or rapidly than in the area of decision-making as it is related to vocational development. Neither are there more dramatic possibilities for an expanded counselor role than in the facilitation of student decision-making and the attendant acquisition of such personal characteristics as vocational identity, self understanding, and personal responsibility. Vocational development as used in this context is more than occupational choice, more than that which is specific to students leaving school and going directly into the labor market. It is instead highly related to personal development and self-acceptance broadly conceived as these goals are appropriate to all students regardless of their ultimate motivational objectives or life styles.

The purposes of this monograph are to examine the interrelationships of decision-making and vocational development; to examine the current approaches to understanding decision-making; to identify the specific effects upon decision-making and vocational development of different personal characteristics; and, finally, to suggest some of the ways by which school counselors can influence positively the process of vocational development among all students in the educational enterprise.

E. L. H.

1

Decision-Making and
Vocational Development

Decision-making and vocational development are rubrics which represent concerns of high priority to the guidance and counseling practitioner. Research and conceptual designs deriving from or converging on these terms pervade the professional literature. Certainly, from a historical perspective, guidance in all its ramifications has been concerned consistently with assisting individuals to plan, to choose, to decide. In terms of counseling, Goldman (1961) has stated that: "An almost universal characteristic . . . is that it deals with decisions and plans . . . counseling is usually to give help in making decisions and plans for the future and in choosing among alternative courses of action in the world of reality." There is no evidence that individual or group needs for assistance in making plans or deciding upon choices will abate in the foreseeable future. Man must make choices. Indeed, human development, i.e. the process of an individual's becoming, consists largely of his decisions and subsequent courses of action (Zaccharia, 1969).

Yet, what do these terms, decision-making and vocational development, mean in other than an abstract sense? How are they related? How can they inform the professional behavior of those charged with facilitating decision-making or vocational development in an individual

1

or in some collective segment of the population? It sometimes appears that the ways by which the individual and his options, vocational and other, may be brought together through guidance or counseling strategies "have been variously taken for granted, obscured, or confined to rational comparison of circumscribed specifications of 'work characteristics' and 'job requirements'" (Pritchard, 1962), even while there abound inquiries and findings which are forming a solid base to broaden and to direct such activities. Thus, it is the purpose of this monograph to examine the terms decision-making and vocational development, to identify the major theoretical conceptions within which they are presently given emphasis, to identify those for whom theory is descriptive or for whom theoretical attention is yet lacking, and to identify guidance strategies by which vocational development and decision-making can be facilitated.

Decision-Making: Process, Event, Outcome or Goal?

While decision-making and choosing are used more or less synonymously, they have come to be used in different contexts to designate a process, an event, an outcome, or a goal. Tiedeman (1961) has wedded the *process* of decision and of vocational development in such observations as the following: "The compromise inherent in discovering and nourishing the area of congruence of person and society as expressed in an individual's vocational behavior is effected within a set of decisions. The set of decisions and the context of relevance for the anticipation and implementation of each constitutes the essence of vocational development." Thus, vocational development subsumes a series of decisions, many with direct connection to vocational content and others less directly connected but no less important. Dilley (1965) has also reported relationships between vocational maturity and decision-making ability. He notes that indices such as acceptance of responsibility, concern with choice, specificity of information, specificity of planning, extent of planning, and the use of resources correlate significantly with measures of decision-making ability and vocational maturity as well as with intelligence, achievement, and participation in extracurricular activities.

When used in the sense of *event*, a behavior occurring at a point in time, "a vocational decision is defined as any behavior that consistently and significantly relates to eventual participation in an occupation" (Miller, 1968). But, choice is rarely considered spontaneous or without antecedents. As Holland (1959) observes:

at the time of vocational choice the person is the product of the interaction of his particular heredity with a variety of cultural and personal
forces including peers, parents and significant adults, his social class,
American culture, and the physical environment. Out of this experience
the person develops a hierarchy of habitual or preferred methods for
dealing with environmental tasks . . . the person making a vocational
choice in a sense searches for situations which satisfy his hierarchy of
adjustive orientations.

Bordin, Nachman and Segal (1963) have indicated that a particular
choice should be seen as a subgoal in a continuous process, but that a
particular choice is not synonymous with the end of the process.

Decision-making can be considered an *outcome* when it results from
or is the product of some guidance strategy — e.g. counseling, group
activity, providing information. Frequently, such outcomes are ascribed
some value. Thus, a good decision is considered to be one whose outcomes (results) are favorable. The problem is that judgments about
whether or not a decision is a "good" one are typically made not by the
chooser but by some external "expert." Consequently, such judgments
may have no relationship to anything that the decision-maker himself
values (Dilley, 1967). This observation in no way vitiates the expectation that the making of decisions ought to result from student interaction with guidance strategies. It rather suggests that value judgments are more tenuously applied to decision events than to decision
processes. In the latter instance, Dilley (1967) has suggested three
possible criteria for "good" decision-making which blends a process
view and a direct base in individual values; that the individual:
(1) chooses the alternative whose expected outcome has the highest
probability coupled with the highest desirability, (2) is internally
consistent, and (3) is willing to assume personal responsibility for the
decision. In a similar vein, decision-making can also be considered a
goal of the counselor as reflected in professional function statements,
e.g., "to assist each pupil to meet the needs to develop personal decision-
making competency" (APGA, 1964). To accomplish such a goal one
must assume that there are inherent in the making of decisions, skills
which guidance strategies or counseling can help one to acquire; or,
as Clarke, Gelatt, and Levine (1965) observe "an effective strategy for
analyzing, organizing, and synthesizing information in order to make
a choice."

What, then, are the components of decision-making whether conceived as process, event, outcome, or goal? Decisions do not have in-
tegrity outside of a context within which a decision is relevant; they do
not operate in isolation. This is explicit in Tyler's (1961) identification

of some of the characteristics of decision-making sessions which includes:

1. The first thing the client needs to achieve is a sense of the general direction he wishes to go, the purposes that the decision he makes must serve for him.

2. After this or along with it he must consider the *limits* of the situation within which his free choice operates.

3. Knowing what he wants and understanding the limitations that are placed upon him, the individual can narrow down the range of possibilities open to him, thus cutting down on the amount of confusion.

While such an analysis helps set the direction for counselor-counselee interaction, it does little to help understand the components of a decision per se. It does suggest, however, that within deliberations about decision-making there are at least three questions: (1) To what extent is the choice predetermined? (2) How does an individual make a choice? (3) Within what limitations of the social environment is his choice made? (Overs, 1964) All of these questions will be addressed throughout this text, but at this point it is important to recognize that freedom of choice has both internal and external concomitants. For example, the factors of free and informed choice which are extrinsic to the individual within educational settings find expression in contextual as well as in social permissiveness. Contextual permissiveness is manifested in the degree of possible access to existing curricula as well as in the availability of curricula that are responsive to where individual students are in their search for pathways to particular goals. In addition, however, free choice of curriculum or free choice of vocational options can exist only when the social structure, i.e. teachers, parents, counselor, the community at large, ascribes equal value to the differential options available to the student (social permissiveness) (Herr, 1969). But, in addition to contextual or social permissiveness, another major aspect of freedom of choice lies within the individual himself. The internal concomitants of free choice are dependent upon the self-knowledge one has, and the degree to which such knowledge is reflected, integrated, and freely used in behavior.

As the research spotlight has been applied to decision-making, mathematical descriptions of human behavior in highly goal-directed kinds of activity or in situations when choices are to be made among a number of known alternatives have been adapted from game or decision theory (Blocher, 1966a). The notion is simply that a student has several possible "alternatives" or courses of action among which to choose. In each of them certain "events" can occur. Each of these events has a "value" for the student, a value which can be estimated through some variant of psychological scaling. Each event also has associated with it a probability of its occurrence which can be estimated through actuarial prediction. If for each course of action, the value of each event is multiplied by its probability, and if these products are summed for each alternative, then the sound decision from this point of view would be for the student to choose the alternative in which the sum of the expected "values" is the greatest (Hills, 1964).

Brayfield (Brayfield and Crites, 1964) would add that formal decision theory suggests that choice is seen as occurring under conditions of uncertainty or risk. The individual assigns a reward value (utility) to alternative choices and appraises his chances of being able to realize each of them (subjective probability). As a result, it is postulated that the individual will attempt to maximize the expected value in making a decision. That the concept of subjective probabilities is crucial to decision-making has been persuasively asserted by Thoresen and Mehrens (1967). They state that "objective probabilities are not directly involved in the decision-making process, but are only involved insofar as they are related to subjective probabilities. The question that arises is the extent to which certain information (objective probability data) actually influences what the person thinks are his chances (subjective probability) of an outcome occurring." Thus, although formal decision theory conceives of decision-making as (1) a process, (2) having an essentially rational-base, and (3) involving the selection of a single alternative at a particular point in time (Costello & Zalkind, 1963), it is necessary to exert great caution in accepting the rationality of decisions as a truism. Indeed, as Hansen (1964–65) has pointed out, decisions are frequently more psychological than logical. In a succinct summary of the points expressed here, Blau, Gustad, Jessor, Parnes and Wilcock (1956) contend that: "A choice between various possible courses of action can be conceptualized as motivated by two interrelated sets of factors: the individual's valuation of different alternatives and his appraisal of his chances of being able to realize each of the alternatives."

Within the valuation of alternatives, Tillinghast (1964) contends that planning and deciding by the counselee and the counselor inevitably include some combination of choice orientations concerned with (1) the probable, (2) the possible and (3) the desirable. Consideration of, and concern with, the *probable* emphasizes alternatives stressing security, stability, and safety, e.g., those jobs which are likely to remain relatively unaffected by the changing times, colleges with admission requirements safely within the demonstrated scholastic ability level of the counselee, emotional and social expressions of the counselee which are safely within the boundary of "socially sanctioned utterances." This orientation defines what is best for the individual in terms of the numerical advantage for success. A choice orientation toward the *possible* holds that the rewards of success are more important than the consequences of failures; thus, factors of danger, erratic and vague influences, excitement and unpredictable events are not things to be avoided in trying to maximize security. In this context, the counselor is concerned with what the individual *might be* and emphasizes widening the counselee's perceptual field with respect to choices and plans. Alternatives emphasizing the *desirable* are not what *could be* or even what *might be*, but what *must* or *should be*. This choice orientation gives little attention to statistical reality as it now exists or future situations as they can be reasonably projected. Tillinghast (1964) suggests that counselees of this orientation are likely to be described as *dedicated, single-minded,* or even *unrealistic* but he also maintains on their behalf that to consider only those courses of action in which the odds for success are 95 out of 100 (probable) is to deny a large portion of life's potential.

Implicit in the previous exploration of the probable, possible, and the desirable is the importance of one's occupational aspirations. There are basically two types of individual aspirations, ideal and real. The ideal aspiration expresses what a person would most like to achieve; the real aspiration expresses what he believes that he will in fact achieve. The closer the real aspiration approximates the ideal aspiration, the less internal conflict an individual experiences (Henderson, 1966). Several decision theorists (Davidson, Suppes and Siegel, 1957) describe the process of making a decision between uncertain outcomes as requiring reconciliation of several general factors: the relative valuing of the outcomes, the cost of attaining the outcomes, and the probability that each outcome may occur. This approach, similar to what Hilton (1962) has labeled "probable gain," includes the dimension of investment. It suggests that within any choice or decision the individual must assess his resources and how much of them, tangible or psychological, he wants to commit to a particular alternative in such a manner as to maximize his gain and minimize his loss. "A vital facet of the decision-making process involves a consideration of the requirements, rewards, and duties inherent in the several available alternatives at the point of choice as balanced with considerations of personal capacities, interest, and values" (Garbin, 1967).

Katz (1966) has suggested, in a model of guidance for career decision-making, that an index of "investment" be developed to represent the substance of what a student risks or loses in preparing for or electing any available career option. This assumes that the student can be helped to determine the "odds," the chances of success in entering or attaining some alternative. More importantly, however, it means that knowing the odds is insufficient for decision-making. The student must also assess the importance to himself of success in each option or the seriousness of failure. To make such assessments immediately places one's decisions in a value domain. Thus, decision-making includes the identifying and the defining of one's values, what they are and what they are not, where they appear and where they do not appear. An initial step for counselor and counselee is to ascertain within the context of a particular decision the relevant value dimensions, to create a hierachy of value factors relevant to the student's uniqueness and the specific kind of decision being considered.

Decisions, then, are not isolated from one's self-concepts. The weighing of choices cannot be accomplished in generalities; it is done in the specific. "Identifying alternatives before him, the person must take stock of himself" (Samler, 1968). Samler maintains that it is well to focus on decision-making as learning and on counseling as training in decision-making because in his vocational life the individual faces not one decision point, but a number. As a continuing product of technological change, such a need will become more pertinent to the individual. The problem, then, is one of creating in a counselee a basic belief in identifying and weighing both the alternatives and the factors in his life pertinent to each alternative.

While it has been generally accepted that vocational decision-making is a process of zeroing in on a sequentially narrower parameter of jobs or job clusters, a convergence from a wide to a narrow range of job possibilities (Kunze, 1967), increasing evidence is accumulating that choice is an effort to implement the self-concept. But implementing the self-concept through available choices is not necessarily to be seen as perpetuating the *status quo*. Rather, implementing the self-concept may be more appropriately seen, in some instances, as an opportunity to actualize the self (Wheeler and Carnes, 1968) through experiences which will cause one's talents, capacities and interests to be expanded.

Most of the decision elements described assume the presence of personal and environmental information necessary to the choice. It is also assumed that the decision itself is a positive step in the solution of a problem, whether the problem is deciding upon how one will spend his life in the vocational sense or how he can obtain access to some educational endeavor preceding commitment to a life work. Zytowski (1965) and Gross (1967), in particular, have sounded cautionary notes about the realism of and the availability of pertinent information as well as about viewing all decisions as positive in direction. Zytowski (1965) has discussed the need for consideration of avoidance behavior as an important force in vocational development. Gross (1967), in a similar but more comprehensive approach, has applied the concept of "disjointed incrementalism" to vocational development. He suggests that: "decisions are always made on the basis of very limited knowledge and typically involve a relatively small change from an existing state of affairs. . . . Further, the choice process is a jagged operation consisting of a series of steps, reversible in many places, and marked often by the adjustment of ends to means. . . . Persons do not first look at the ends that they seek to attain and then go about looking for means. Rather the means are already settled by the resources that the individual has available or by his skills. He therefore looks for ends that can be attained by the resources he has." In this conception, "instead of thinking of a choice as moving *toward* a solution of a problem, it is thought of as moving *away* from a situation that is undesirable . . . one seeks not to eliminate a problem but to alleviate it."

Finally, it is important to recognize that decisions imply action. Thus, within the concept of decision-making there are behaviors which operate prior to or concurrent with deciding upon a course of action and there are behaviors which are inherent in implementing the decision and the action which the decision directs. Tiedeman (1961) maintains that with regard to *each* decision, "the problem of deciding may be profitably divided into two *periods* or aspects, a period of *anticipation* and a period of *implementation* or *adjustment*." He further analyzes anticipatory behavior into subaspects or stages which include: exploration, crystallization and choice, and specification. In *exploration*, the alternatives or goals which the individual considers determine the field from which choice will eventually emerge. During this stage, the person considers his interests, capabilities, the opportunities available to him now and their relationship to the future as they can affect him and his dependents, and his level of tolerance for the requirements characteristic of each alternative.

During the period of exploration, Tiedeman indicates that "a person attempts to take the 'measure' of himself in relation to each alternative as he senses it" (Tiedeman, 1961). In the stage of *crystallization*, which follows in more specific fashion the stage of exploration, the individual orders his self "measures" and the relevant considerations in each of the goals previously considered. This is a time when sequences of tentative crystallizations, new explorations, and recrystallizations operate. As the *choice* becomes imminent, crystallizations stabilize and a particular goal is elected which orients the behavior pertinent to the choice. At this point, the degree of certainty, of rationality, and the residual appeal of alternatives not selected each combine to give strength to the motive power by which specification will ensue. Specification, which is the stage immediately prior to the act by which the choice is implemented, is a time when one's self image absorbs the implications of the choice and doubts concerning the viability of the decision are assuaged.

Tiedeman (1961) also breaks the period of implementation and adjustment into stages which include induction, transition, and maintenance. These stages describe the behaviors which are likely to occur when one confronts the reality of implementing the choice. It is here that the congruence of one's expectations and the expectations of the context in which the choice will be implemented are tested. During the stage of introduction, the individual will receive feedback from his superiors and his colleagues about how he is expected to behave in the role set for him, and he will modify his self-image or expectations accordingly; or, he will reinstitute the period of anticipation on his way to leaving the scene. If the individual handles successfully the stage of induction, he will move through a period of transition in which his behavior will be reoriented from receptivity to assertiveness. He will take into his self-image, in an increasingly perfected way, the modified expectations and goals implied by the role definitions to which he has been exposed and he will reciprocate by reshaping some of the expectations held by the environment. Finally, with such modification of both the individual and the group expectations the maintenance phase will be initiated. This stage is described by Tiedeman (1961) as a period of "dynamic equilibrium" which can be altered by changes in the ordering and the orientations of the internal or external stimuli by which the equilibrium is constituted.

Tiedeman's (1961) conception of decision-making as action oriented is supported by other researchers and theorists yet to be discussed. But the essence of the point is captured by the following observation (Calia, 1966b): "It is not only what the student selects out of the myriad of stimuli to which he is exposed that is important, but it is what he does with them after he has made his selection that is highly significant."

Summary

In summary, then, this selection has attempted to identify some of the meanings for the use of the term decision-making and some of the elements which are encompassed by this term. It seems clear that although a decision may seem discrete, it is really only a step in a series of previously made decisions. It is influenced by multiple factors which include: (1) personal variables such as aptitudes, interests, sex, age, physical strength, and personal history; (2) social and cultural factors, which operate on an impersonal basis, including societal values and other norms, job requirements, and employment opportunities; (3) interpersonal relationships received by the decision-maker; and, (4) the relevance of the decision-maker's reference groups (Slocum, 1965).

Vocational Development

Until fairly recently, the classic problem for those involved in the vocational aspects of guidance or counseling has been that of predicting or helping individuals to predict occupational choice or occupational success. Such a goal is a residual of Parsonian "True Reasoning" by which are matched the traits of men and occupations through modifications of actuarial procedure. If one is seeking the choice of an occupation, defined primarily as the ability to perform a narrowly defined set of tasks, one can be comfortable with concentrating upon a specific choice point. However, current conceptions of vocational development or career development, typically used synonymously, respond not to occupations narrowly defined but rather to careers. "A career is the *sequence* of occupations, jobs, and positions in the life of an individual whether these are or are not vertically and laterally related" (Super, 1961). The emphasis in the psychological or sociological study of *careers* is on the continuities and discontinuities in the lives of individuals and on the similar patterns in the lives of groups (Super, 1954) whereas in the psychology and sociology of occupations the emphasis is on the characteristics of occupations as revealed by the people in them (Super, 1964a).

As developmental psychology and occupational sociology have in their own right moved toward maturity, it has become clear that it is possible "to view human development and the quest for maturity through a vocational prism" (Borow 1961). Thus, theories and research conceived to examine vocational or career development are, in reality, a "search for the psychological meaning of vocationally relevant acts (including the exploratory vocational behavior of youth) and of work itself in the human experience" (Borow, 1961). Within this context, recent theories of vocational development view vocational behavior as a continuing and fluid process of growth and learning. And, they attach considerable importance to the individual's self-concept(s), developmental experiences, and psycho-social environment as major determinants of this process.

As related to the earlier discussion of decision-making, it is essentially accurate to state that vocational development is concerned with the factors which motivate or impede and which trigger specific decisions. But, "vocational development not only occurs within the context of a single decision; vocational development ordinarily occurs within the context of several decisions. . . . Each decision is also to be considered in relation with a wider context of past and future decisions leading to the presentation of career. . . ." (Tiedeman, 1961). Thus, vocational development is intimately linked with the sets of decisions and their outcomes by which the character of the process is defined. "Vocational development may be conceived of as a decision-making process which creates two trends: (a) narrowing the range of possibilities, and (b) strengthening the possibilities which remain. Through the successive refinement of these trends, events are experienced, construed and acted upon until a career choice is arrived at" (Hershenson and Roth, 1966).

The interaction of persons with the situational circumstances in which they find themselves also relates to the behavioral repertoire which they will accumulate. Ivey and Morrill (1968) state:

> Career process may be defined as the continuing process through which a person engages in the sequence of developmental tasks necessary for personal growth in occupational life . . . those searching for a career should be seen not as individuals hunting for a place in a stable society, but as changing organisms engaging in a series of career-related developmental tasks that enable them to adapt themselves to a changing society.

In actuality, there is not one concept of developmental tasks but several (Zaccharia, 1965). For example, there is a conception of developmental tasks attuned to general development and defined as: "a task which arises at or about a certain period in the life of the individual; successful achievement of which leads to happiness and success with later tasks, while failure leads to unhappiness in the individual, disapproval by society, and difficulty with later tasks" (Havighurst, 1953).

There are also developmental task formulations directly tied to vocational behavior as described by Super and his colleagues (Super, Starishevsky, Matlin and Jordaan, 1963), and those which from a psychoanalytic persuasion are the outcomes of psycho-social crises (Erikson, 1959). While each of these conceptualizations of developmental tasks has about it a nomothetic, modal, or average quality, they each have idiographic or individual importance. As Zaccharia has pointed out (1965) each developmental task has a unique meaning to each individual as mediated by his value, attitude or need system. Secondly, individuals vary with respect to their general approach, e.g., — hesitating, eager, methodical, casual — to developmental tasks influenced by such personal traits as age, sex, temperament as well as cultural factors such as socio-economic class. Finally, individuals vary in their patterns of mastering developmental tasks according to their capacities and the experiential opportunities which they have been provided. LoCascio (1964) has identified three basic patterns for mastering developmental tasks which result from the differential interaction of individual-environmental characteristics: continuous, delayed, and impaired. Similarly, Masik (1967) studied the concept of *Career Saliency* as a means of indicating the importance to persons of a career and the factors which differentiate the relative strength of such a concern. He defined *Career Saliency* as: (a) the degree to which a person is career motivated, (b) the degree to which an occupation is important as a source of satisfaction, and (c) the degree of priority ascribed to occupation among other sources of satisfactions.

As vocational development theory and research has incorporated the developmental task concept, it has also placed increasing emphasis on the staging of development. Within a framework of life stages, Ginsberg, Ginsberg, Axelrad, and Herma (1951) suggested three stages in the choice process which were intimately related to the evolving of interests, capacities, and values: fantasy (below age 11); tentative (ages 11 to 17); and realistic (above age 17). Super (1957) identified five stages of vocational development: growth (conception to age 14); exploration (ages 15 to 24); establishment (ages 25 to 44); maintenance (ages 45 to 64); and decline (ages 65 and above). Each of these stages has sub-stages and meta-dimensions which are mediated by both personal and cultural factors. Hershenson (1968), using an application of energy utilization to vocational modes, suggested the following: Social-Amniotic (awareness → being); Self-Differentiation (control → play); Competence (Directed → work); Independence (Goal-directed → occupation) and Commitment (Invested → vocation). Havighurst (1964) identified six stages of vocational development as including: identification with a worker (ages 5 to 10); acquiring the habits of industry (10–15); acquiring identity as a worker in the occupational structure (15–25); maintaining a productive person (25–40); maintaining a productive society (40–70); and contemplating a productive and responsible life (70 and above). Miller and Form (1951) described vocational development stages as including the following: preparatory (birth to age 14), initial (14 to the end of formal or full-time education); trial (from school leaving to age 34); stable (35 to retirement); and retirement (retirement to death).

While there are additional conceptions of the stages phenomenon in vocational development, those cited are sufficient to emphasize the point that development in a vocational sense is not isolated from general development; it is really a special case of the latter. Indeed, one can conceive of current theories of vocational behavior as being limited, specific statements of general theories of motivation. Further, vocational development is mediated by the education and social systems of which one is a part not only in adolescence and in adulthood but in the early years of life. Choices and expectations are built into these systems, and they are not uniformly distributed through or demanded by all strata of society. To apply universally developmental psychology in its concern for individual differences as the most important prism for viewing differences in vocational development, is insufficient without also giving credence to cultural determinants.

The preceding discussion of developmental tasks and life stages emphasizes that vocational behavior is complex and dynamic. It is the result of a reciprocal process, experience interacting with preconceptions eventuating in change and vocational development.

> The essence of development is progressive increase and modification of the individual's behavioral repertoire through growth and learning . . . the individual in his development, develops bit by bit. Each step in his development not only has bearing upon, but indeed is the basis of each succeeding stage. . . . Thus, the nature of the development in each step or stage is determined by prior ones and by the environmental factors and their interaction with the individual while he is progressing through them. (Super, Crites, Hummel, Moser, Overstreet, and Warnath, 1957)

Intimately associated with the development framework is that of vocational maturity which assumes that vocational behavior changes systematically with age. As one becomes older, his vocational behavior becomes more goal-directed, more realistic, and more independent. He moves in increments from flux to stabilization, from diffusion to specification, from fantasy to reality. Evidence has begun to accumulate that vocationally mature individuals are more mature not only in occupational attitudes and orientations, but also in personality characteristics, further strengthening the linkage between vocational maturity and general personality development (Bohn, 1966).

Vocational development is also seen as an expression of personality (Holland, 1966b). It is increasingly viewed as a continuing attempt to implement one's evolving self-concept. At specific points in life one is called upon to state, explicitly or implicitly, through the choices made that "I am this but not that kind of person." Simons (1966) contends, from an existential point of view, that vocational choice is ultimately a result of an array of decisions, major and minor, leading to self-objectification. It is these sequential decisions which give the individual the option of standing out as fully responsible before his fellow man, of being objectified, or of conforming to certain stereotypes which permit him to escape the painful process of having others see him as he really is. Hence, it is the ego strength which one builds and commits to these decisions that ultimately determines whether he is going to spend his life in dynamically realizing his potential, or spend it in the frustration of fighting his own innate drive toward fulfillment. This is the raw material of which vocational maturity and personality are made.

If vocational development is an expression of personality and an attempt to implement an evolving self-concept, then it is reasonable to see it as a focus of the identity search. "In our society one of the most clear-cut avenues through which identity concerns are expressed is the process of making a vocational choice. . . . Choosing a vocation involves a kind of public self-definition that forces one to say to the world, 'This is what I am'" (Galinsky and Fast, 1966). Thus, problems in resolving the identity crisis are frequently perceived by "significant others" as difficulties in choosing a vocation particularly as manifested in vocational indecision. Such an insight obviously has implications for where the counselor begins and how he helps the counselee conceive of his dilemma. While perhaps there is only a subtle difference between implementation of a self-concept and actualization of an ideal self there is evidence that vocational development or the choices by which such development is defined may be a vehicle for actualization. Thus, the relationships found in recent studies (Pallone and Hosinski, 1967; Wheeler and Carnes, 1968) between ideal self-concepts and perceptions of occupational role expectations as opposed to relationships between the present self and such expectations supports the potential viability of vocational development as self-actualization. To perceive the intent of vocational development as, at least for some individuals, a personal attempt to achieve self-actualization and self-enhancement, seems tenable if for no other reason than that sociologists have found pervasive connections between one's career sequence or occupation and his entire "way of life" or "life cycle" (Cohen, 1964). As Super has asserted (1957), "work and occupation play an important part in determining the social status, values, attitudes and style of living of an individual. Important though some of these are as determinants of occupation, they in turn are partly determined by occupation. Occupation is not merely a means of earning a *livelihood,* but also a *way* of *life,* a social role."

Summary

This section has attempted to place into perspective the current emphases in vocational development theory as they link decisions and vocational behavior. Further, it has stressed that one's occupation can be placed in a larger fabric of vocation, of one's purpose in or commitment to life. Vocational development theory is creating a frame of reference for counselors in which a broader range of variables and the hierarchies of interaction they represent are being cast in an extended time perspective having implications for the application of guidance strategies not only at a particular choice point but during the periods of development before or between points of decision.

2

Theories of Vocational Development and Decision-Making

As Brayfield (Brayfield and Crites, 1964) has pointed out, the term "theory" as applied to vocational development is somewhat pretentious if intended in the strictest sense. He is not alone in this observation. Carkhuff, Alexik and Anderson (1967) applied a schema for the inductive and deductive functions of theory-building to the contributions of most of the conceptions which follow and their conclusion was that none of the dominant approaches satisfy the established criteria of theory-building. Others like Stefflre (1966) and LoCascio (1967) have also raised important questions about the present state of vocational development theory.

Without gainsaying the observations of these critics of the current state of theory, it is nevertheless all we have. If one views the dominant approaches which follow with a less than jaundiced eye, one quickly senses that while no one approach yields the comprehensiveness of explanation one might wish, collectively there exists a conceptual frame of reference which views vocational development and decision-making through the lenses of many disciplines. There is emerging a set of constructs and propositions, some tested and some not, which serve to explain differential decision behavior and trends in the vocational aspects of development.

Brayfield has also indicated that there is an intermediate strategy which falls between empiricism and the building of theory. "It calls for the development and application of a conceptual framework in the classic tradition of the experimentalist who attempts to identify with precision and clarity the major dependent and independent variables involved in his problem and works from there to an understanding of functional dependencies" (Brayfield and Crites, 1964). That is about where we are now. Brayfield further notes that such a framework has at least four virtues: (1) It provides an immediately useful orientation for the practitioner, (2) It forces a comprehensive consideration of the great range of variables involved, (3) It points to the hard, back-breaking row the researcher must hoe if we are to have a substantial basis for practice, and it dramatically establishes the limits of our present knowledge, and (4) Finally, the systematic investigation of the operation of relevant variables makes more likely the formulation of theoretical constructs that are tied to reality and are thus potentially more useful to the practitioner.

Because knowledge about vocational development is still incomplete, even though theoretical and research efforts are multiplying in geometric progression, it seems necessary to take the broadest possible view of the approaches available. Just as denominational shadings sometimes cause the search for theological truths to be viewed through different prisms, so it is with the search for understanding of vocational development. The characteristics peculiar to the particular theoretician or researcher — whether these be the discipline he espouses, the breadth or narrowness of his preparation or any other combination of factors either intrinsic or extrinsic — will cause him to order and interpret information in a specific way and with a specific emphasis. This is in no way a negative observation. It is rather a generalization of the phenomenological approach to understanding behavior: "That one behaves as one perceives" (Snygg & Combs, 1949). Because of our specific developmental histories, we do not all interpret any given event in quite the same fashion. Consequently, any specific event can cause to be generated an array of behavior in the people exposed to it. At the same time, an array of different stimuli can cause the same overt behavior in those persons exposed to the stimuli. Hence, explanations of behavior stem from many perceivers and analyzers, each having his own lens through which he views the complexities to which he directs his attention.

The approaches which describe vocational development or some piece of it have been classified in several ways. As comprehensive as any, are those by Hilton and by Osipow. Hilton (1962) has classified five possible approaches to the decision-making process into the Attribute Matching Model, the Need Reduction Model, the Economic Man Model, the Social Man Model, and the Complex Information Processing Model. Osipow (1968) has placed career development theory into four categories: trait-factor approaches, sociology and career choice, self-concept theory, and vocational choice and personality theories. Since both the classifications of Hilton and of Osipow discuss generally the same body of knowledge or speculation, they will be blended together in this chapter.

Theories of Vocational Development and Decision-Making

Trait-Factor or Actuarial

The trait-factor or actuarial theory of vocational choice is the oldest, most persistent, and most straightforward of the approaches pervading theory, research and practice in vocational development. Its logic is reflected in the assumptions that (1) individual differences can be observed and classified in terms of certain variables — e.g., interests and abilities; (2) occupational requirements and characteristics can be classified in an analogous way; (3) the individual can match himself or be matched to the "right" occupation. Once this matching is accomplished, the problem of vocational choice is resolved for the particular individual.

The major criticism of this explanation of choice is that it is too static. It does not provide for or consider the dynamics, the changing nature, of the individual or the environmental situations which will confront him and to which he must relate himself not just once but periodically throughout his life. When carried to the extreme, the limitations of trait and factor theory are reflected in the observation that, "it is analogous to fitting round pegs in round holes with neither the pegs nor the holes remaining round for a consistent period of time." A more important criticism is that trait-and-factor approaches to vocational choice give more credence to man's basic rationality and the primacy of cognitive elements in decision-making and development than do approaches more recently evolved.

Such criticisms, while they cause the practitioner to be wary of embracing the trait-factor approach as his only professional mode, do not imply that this approach has nothing to commend it. It has provided the impetus for appraising individual status on traits found to be of relevance in occupational success, satisfaction, and differentiation as well as in assessing the contribution of individual traits to the accomplishment of specific work activities. Interest inventories, aptitude batteries, personality measures, as well as systems for classifying differences in occupations, have largely found their genesis in a trait-factor conception.

Trait and factor theory acquired a strong partnership with the psychometric tradition which began to flourish early in this century. Yet with all the statistical sophistication, testing refinement, and technological application, the resulting differential prediction of individuals finding success in specific occupations has been discouragingly imprecise. Tiedeman (1958), in a review of trait and factor studies relative to predictions of vocational success, concluded that: "In every study, the choice and successful pursuit of a goal has proven to be a function of one's aptitudes, *but* in every instance the most striking feature of the distributions of aptitudes for the people making the various choices was their *overlap*." And, a bit later, Thorndike and Hagen (1959), as a result of a massive actuarial study examining the traits of 10,000 men and the characteristics of the careers in which they were found a decade or more later, wrote: "We should view the long-range prediction of occupational success by aptitude tests with a good deal of skepticism and take a very restrained view as to how much can be accomplished." Each of these individuals is saying that aptitudes and other similar predictors of occupational placement or success are important but not exclusive of other manifestations of personality such as values, energy levels, perseverance, and so on.

If one were to subscribe to the trait and factor approach to choice behavior as the sole description of vocational development and decision-making, one would have to assume a much greater degree of self-insight, not simply with the measurable aspects of the self, but as a wholly functioning organism and the relationships between self and the personally important components of the options among which one can choose, than seems true of most persons (Hilton, 1962). In addition, if one considers the counselor as the major source of information about self characteristics and occupational factors, one must face the possibility that the counselee is accepting such information on the basis of faith in an authority figure. Consequently, the choices he makes are not made as affirmations of identity developed from insights into himself, his feelings, his view of the world, but rather because it is expedient to assume that he will find success in an occupation on the basis of probabilities of success derived from statistical findings that he resembles certain occupational populations.

Economic

An implicit derivation of trait and factor theory which has constituted a strong influence on thinking about decision-making and vocational development is economic in origin. The assumption is made, based upon Keynesian economic theory, that one chooses a career or an occupational goal which will maximize his gain and minimize his loss. The gain or loss is, of course, not necessarily money but might be anything of value to the particular individual. A given occupational or career pathway might be considered as a means of achieving certain possibilities — e.g., great prestige, security, a spouse, social mobility — when compared to another course of action. Implicit here is the expectation that the individual can predict the outcomes of various alternatives as well as the probabilities of each, and that he will then choose that one which promises the most reward for his investment — e.g., time, tuition, union dues, delayed gratification — with the least probability of fear or failure. Such a conception of goal attractiveness and behavior seems pervasive and implicit in the literature of decision-making but it too assumes a rational and logical vocational development which seems fraught with contingency.

Social Structure

It has become increasingly clear that the social structure of which one is a part has a great deal to do with the viability of the choices which one makes. A recent label, the Culture of Poverty, has invaded both the popular and professional literature dealing with vocational development. Evolving from a base in sociology, it describes the special circumstances that shape the lives of the poor and separate them from their affluent fellow citizens. The conditions in which poverty flourishes produce a distinctive milieu that conditions the social responses, the educational attainment, the vocational ambition, and the general level of intellectual competence of the overwhelming majority of those raised within its stifling precincts (Moynihan, 1964). To live in poverty over generations produces a personality of impovershiment.

The major premise of a social structure approach to vocational development or decision-making relates to the limitations placed upon career selection by restrictive social class horizons. Much floundering in decision-making is a result of limited avenues through which one can implement choice or of limitations upon the knowledge of opportunities available to the individual so restricted. Caplow (1954) as well as Miller and Form (1951) among others have discussed the accident theory of vocational development which stresses the importance of circumstances external to the individual dictating his possibilities for occupational choice and purposeful development. The individual of restricted social support may blunder into or find himself in jobs without any consistent potential for growth or advancement, for career in its most positive connotation, because the only guideline available is immediate gratification. Hence, the narrowness or the breadth of the individual's cultural or social class horizons has much to do with the choices he can make, can consider, or can implement. While the personal aspirations of an individual raised in an environment which does not support planfulness or long-term commitments may be the same in a global sense as those held by a contemporary in more favored circumstances, it is doubtful that the former has the knowledge or the techniques by which he can cope effectively with his environment to realize the aspirations he holds. While accurate and relevant information is not all there is to a good decision or the fine grain of vocational development, for disadvantaged students faced with narrow role models in the family and limited social horizons in the immediate community, it is doubtful that decisions will be made or that long term development will ensue without appropriate information or the psychological support to accept the personal realities of it. Because of recent Federal or State legislation and growing social enlightenment, freedom of choice in occupational and educational avenues is on the rise and the overt and covert social restrictions placed upon many individuals based upon arbitrary stands of suitability as defined by class or race or religious creed are crumbling. Yet, an increasingly open social structure is viable only if the individuals previously blocked can muster the required personal resources, the internal elements of freedom of choice, to engage successfully the emerging avenues of access to the mainstream of occupational opportunities through which personal career processing and vocational development find fruition. While the effects of the social structure upon individual choice-making appear most devastating among the disadvantaged, to a large extent the same variables operate at the opposite end of the social structure to cause economically favored youth to view in a very restricted sense the opportunities which are suitable to their circumstances.

Complex-Information Processing

A fourth approach to decision-making, which has particular relevance to the outcomes of premature choosing and the resulting restrictions upon the fullest realization of vocational development, lies in what has been called complex information processing (Hilton, 1962). Hilton contends that the "reduction of dissonance among a person's beliefs about himself and his environments is the major motivation of career decision-making." He takes his lead from Festinger's Theory of Cognitive Dissonance (1957) which indicates that the magnitude of information, the number of factors which should be considered, in decision-making is so great that the individual makes a choice prematurely, without full consideration of the implications of the choice, in order to reduce the pressures besieging him as he sorts through the torrents of information relevant to the choice. He then reinforces the efficacy of the choice by rationalization: selective attention to those subsequent data which make the choice look good both to the chooser and to external observers. This phenomenon can be represented by a common defense mechanism to which many of us fall prey in purchasing a new automobile. When the new car stimulus gets entrenched in our psyche, whatever its motivation, we are prone to hear noises in our old vehicle which were not there previously, the tires look a bit more bald and we filter from newspaper articles those which suggest that new car prices and taxes will rise in the near future (Herr and Cramer, 1968). All of these elements congeal to soothe our troubled and conflicted concerns about buying the new car when we really know that we can not afford it and that the old vehicle still has a lot of "good" mileage remaining. So it is with some vocationally oriented decisions. Although the chooser knows there are other options with which he could relate in a more compatible manner, particularly over the longer range, it is comforting to make a selection and suppress the costs of its unrealism by a variety of self-deceptive devices.

Reprise for the Counselor

As this analysis of theoretical approaches to decision-making and vocational development proceeds it should be coming clear that, because of the unique history of each individual, these phenomena wear many faces. Thus, any individual must be encouraged and assisted to determine, at any given choice point, What kind of decision is involved? How will required choices fit into the process of vocational development? What are the factors that make a difference to him? These are the relevant questions which will cause one's personal hierarchy of needs and values to be cast in bold relief.

The approaches to which the remainder of this chapter will be devoted can be classified in a number of ways. In the professional literature, they fall under rubrics like "psycho-analytic," "cultural-psychodynamic," "need-reduction," "interpersonal relations and need satisfaction," and "self-concept." For our purposes, however, these various possibilities will be considered only as need or self-concept in emphasis. In general, these theories are more comprehensive and integrated than the preceding approaches and they, in some instances, subsume elements of all those described.

Need Theories

Prominent among the proponents of such an approach are those of the psychoanalytic as well as other, less clearly defined, schools of personality. The major assumption of these approaches is that because of differences in personality structure, individuals develop certain need predispositions, satisfaction of which is sought in occupational choices. Thus, different career areas are populated by persons of different need or personality type. These approaches are characterized rather consistently by classifications of personality type or need category which directly or indirectly are related to gratifications available in different classifications of occupations.

Roe (1956), for example, has applied Maslow's theory of prepotent needs to vocational behavior. In a classic work, Maslow (1954) arranged the needs of human beings into a hierarchy in which the emergence of high-order needs is conceived as contingent upon the satisfaction of lower-order, more primitive needs. The needs begin in ascending order with: (1) the physiological needs; (2) the safety needs; (3) the needs for belongingness and love; (4) the needs for importance, respect, self-esteem, independence; (5) the need for information; (6) the need for understanding; (7) the need for beauty; and (8) the need for self-actualization. Roe (1956) suggests that the level of work in which one is found is related to the degree to which one is freed from using work as a hunt for substitute gratifications for unmet needs at rather primitive levels.

Roe has also examined the relationships between early home environments (e.g., rejecting, overprotecting, democratic), personality manifestations, and occupational choice. In her studies of different types of scientists (Roe, 1953) she concluded that personality differences evolving from different child-rearing practices exist and are related to the kinds of interaction that such persons ultimately establish with people, toward others or not toward others, and things. Such differences in interaction or the focus of one's activity are sought by persons in vocational development as a way of accomplishing need satisfaction. She suggests that there are relationships between the psychic energy, genetic propensities and childhood experiences which shape individual styles of behavior and that securing opportunities to express these individual styles is inherent in the choices made and the vocational behavior which ensues. In this sense, occupational choices are processes of self-categorization. The influencing conditions are the strength of the need, the amount of delay between the arousal of the need and its satisfactions, and the value that the satisfaction of the need has in the individual's immediate environment (Osipow, 1968). Roe's concern with specific child-rearing practices, the manner in which the parents interact with the child, and the resulting orientation toward or away from persons has been translated into a useful field and level occupational classification which includes the following: (Roe, 1956)

Groups	Levels
I. Service	1. Professional and Managerial 1
II. Business Contact	2. Professional and Managerial 2
III. Organizations	3. Semi-Professional, Small Business
IV. Technology	4. Skilled
V. Outdoor	5. Semi-Skilled
VI. Science	6. Unskilled
VII. General Cultural	
VIII. Arts and entertainment	

Thus, as an example, persons in service occupations are primarily oriented toward persons and probably come from homes which generated a loving, over-protecting environment. The level, as reflected in complexity and responsibility, within the service occupation which will be attained is dependent upon the person's intelligence as well as the style applied to environmental manipulation.

A second influential group of spokesmen for a need approach being wedded to vocational development is that stimulated largely by what has been called the Michigan Group. While preceded by Brill's (1948) use of psychoanalytic concepts of guilt and exhibitionism to explain the kind of vocation which people choose, Bordin, Nachman, and Segal (1963), among others of the psychoanalytic persuasion, emphasize the available gratifications which various types of work offer to meet certain individual impulses. They substitute for such common individual traits as interests and abilities, individual modes of impulse gratification, the status of one's psychosexual development, and levels of anxiety.

From occupatioanl analyses of such roles as accountants, creative writers, lawyers, dentists, social workers, clinical psychologists, physicists and engineers, Bordin and his colleagues have conceived an elaborate matrix of basic need-gratifying activities found in different occupations. Thus, they have wedded in meaningful ways concepts such as identification, the development of defense mechanisms, sublimation, and the process of role implementation to personality characteristics and the behavioral gratifications available in varied occupational fields.

Holland's (1966b) evolving approach to vocational choice and development, although not without a psychoanalytic strain, is not confined to any specific theory. In addition to psychoanalytic influences, need theory, role theory, self theory, social learning theory and sociology are each in evidence in his approach. But, because of his classification of personality types and environments in comparable ways it seems appropriate to discuss Holland's work under need theory.

Holland (1966b) assumes that at the time a person chooses his vocation he is a product of his heredity and environment. As a result of these early and continuing influences of genetic potentialities and interactions between the individual and the several elements of his environment, there is developed a hierarchy of habitual or preferred methods for dealing with social and environmental tasks. The most typical way in which an individual responds to his environment is his modal personal orientation. These orientations fall into one of six classifications: realistic, intellectual, social, conventional, enterprising, and artistic. This hierarchy or pattern of personal orientations directs the individual toward an environment that will satisfy his particular hierarchy. Thus, occupational groups furnish different kinds of gratifications or satisfactions which require different abilities, identifications, values, and attitudes. To emphasize the person-situation correspondence, Holland (1966b) has classified work environments into six categories analogous to personal orientations. In other words, he describes the person and the working environment in the same terms. A person's choice of an occupation and his vocational development grow out of expressive acts reflecting his motivations, his knowledge of the occupation in question, his insight and understanding of himself, his personality and abilities. Holland (1966b) makes more explicit than do most of his contemporaries the status of occupations as ways of life, as environments which manifest the characteristics of those inhabiting them as opposed to being simply sets of isolated work functions or skills.

Self-Concept

Self-concept approaches to decision-making and vocational development can be separated from personality approaches not because they reject the latter but because their emphases are more developmentally focused and the importance of the self-concept is dramatized. Conceptions of self have had a central place in these approaches because they serve as at least partial bases for choosing or planning behavior. Self-referents like, "I am not bright enough to go to college," or, "I am strong enough to carry hod," are important, whether accurate or inaccurate, because they prompt the individual to prescribe the limits within which he will function vocationally.

Field, Kehas, and Tiedeman (1963) have suggested that individuals choose actions which fit their current notions of "(1) what they are like; (2) what they can be like; (3) what they want to be like; (4) what their situation is like; (5) what their situation might become; and finally (6) the way they see these aspects of self and situation as being related." Thus, choice is affected by the ways in which the individual arrives at his self-referents as well as by the self-referents themselves.

The self-concept approach which has received the greatest continuing visibility, which has stimulated the most research, and which is the most comprehensive is that promulgated by Super and his colleagues through the Career Pattern Study (Super *et al*, 1957; Super *et al*, 1963). This approach is an integrative one which stresses the interactive nature of personal and environmental variables in the processing of vocational development. Super has made explicit the essential intimacy of vocational development and personal development. He has synthesized much of the early work of Buehler (1933) and of Ginzberg *et al* (1951) in his longitudinal attempt to focus developmental principles on the staging and the determinism of career patterns. He has characterized the career process as ongoing, continuous, and generally irreversible; as a process of compromise and synthesis within which his primary construct, the development and implementation of the self-concept, operates. The basic theme is that the individual chooses occupations whose characteristics will allow him to function in a role that is consistent with his self-concept and that the latter conception is a function of his developmental history. Further, because of the range of individual capabilities and the latitude within occupations for different combinations of traits, he has indicated that most people have multi-potentiality.

Super gives prominence to increasingly complex vocational developmental tasks as these are important at different stages of vocational development. He has formulated gross stages of Crystallization, Specification, Implementation, Stabilization and Consolidation which rest upon sub-stages and meta-dimensions contributing to increasing vocational maturity. Within these stages are factors internal as well as external to the individual which influence the choices made. These factors continue to filter and narrow the array of options the individual considers. There is an emphasis, then, on vocational convergence and greater specificity in behavior.

The work of Tiedeman and O'Hara (1963) like that of Super and his colleagues is concerned with staging and development. They view career development as part of a continuing process of differentiating ego identity. How a person's identity evolves is dependent upon his early childhood experiences with the family unit, the psychosocial crises encountered at various developmental stages, the congruence between society's meaning system and the individual's meaning system as well as the emotional constants of each. Their view of career development as a sequence of developmental life stages or events also is broken into sub-aspects. For example, the aspect of anticipation or preoccupation of career goals includes sub-stages of exploration, crystallization, choice and clarification. Further, in the aspect of implementation or adjustment, there are included steps such as those of social induction, reformation and integration. Pervading these stages are continuing processes of differentiation and integration as outcomes of personality or psychosocial crises which accompany the stages. Tiedeman and O'Hara suggest further that individual personality is shaped by perceptions of career choices and to some degree by the individual's conformance to the norms and values of those individuals already established within the vocational setting. They stress, then, the intimacy of self-concept and career-concept as these develop gradually through many small decisions.

Summary

Approaches to describing and explaining decision-making and vocational development lead to an emphasis on several concepts. First, vocational development like all human behavior is complex. It is integral to the total fabric of personality development. It involves progressive development on the part of those involved, and it is the result of the synthesis of many personal, social, and vocational factors as one matures. Vocational behavior like other behavior develops over time, through processes of growth and learning. Vocational behavior and career selection develop from less effective behavior and unrealistic or fantasy choice to more complex behavior and more realistic choosing. Career selection becomes increasingly reality-oriented and more specific as one moves toward the choice itself. Almost without exception, vocational development theories suppose the existence and causal role of inner, tensional states, which depending upon the focus of the theory, are variously described as interests, needs, values, personality characteristics, or life styles (Zytowski, 1965).

Within vocational development, the measurement and the interpretation of traits are seen as only part of a more comprehensive concern with the totality of personality and the individual self-concept in guided self-appraisal. Static approaches to the study of the individual and of the environment are being modified to reflect continuous change in both and the effect of interaction between them. Specific choices are increasingly seen as intimately tied to an array of choices and developmental tasks demanded by individual development as well as by cultural expectations. The diversity and the importance of values and value systems to vocational choice are receiving increasing recognition.

Since career selection is an ongoing process which extends from infancy through at least young adulthood, the importance of early childhood experiences in the family, the school, and the community are being related to later behavior pertinent to vocational effectiveness. If intervention in facilitating vocational development is to have most impact, vocational development theory supports the need for it to begin during the first decade of life. This is the nursery of human nature and the time when the attitudes are formed which later become manifest in vocational commitment or rejection.

3

Specific Factors in
Vocational Development

As one considers the theories and the definitions which have been presented in Chapters One and Two, with the exception of a few cautionary notes and some brief allusions, it is clear that they are predominantly positive. "They assume that all men want to work, that the idea of a vocation has a positive valence as a goal, or that the effect attached to career behavior is positive" (Zytowski, 1965). While these theories expect or predict that individuals with particular need hierarchies or self-concepts will reject occupations and career patterns that do not seem compatible with these personal expressions, there is little attention given to the possibility that for some persons work is not central to their lives or that it has about it connotations and characteristics that repel rather than attract.

For many persons, vocational development, if that is an appropriate label here, is predicated not on what they want to do but what they do not want to do. They do not say "I want to be a machinist" or "I want to work in an office." Rather, they state emphatically that they will not work in an office, they will not move from their present locale, and that they will not work in a job where the boss is constantly looking over their shoulder. For these people vocational choice seems to be more nearly described as moving away from an undesirable situation in contrast to moving toward an ideal state (Gross, 1967). For other persons, work is not the central commitment for investment of identification or energy that many theoretical postulates assume.

The concept of career is an emotionally charged concept. In the sense that career is seen as entry into a position at the lowest rung of a career ladder followed by an orderly sequence of promotions to positions at successively higher status levels (Slocum, 1965), it is considered in public terms as "good" and virtuous. Yet, such orderly progression is possible within only some strata of the occupational structure — not all. "The work histories of most American men indicate that their work lives have been characterized by lack of commitment to a specific occupation. There is a high probability that most of the pivotal occupational decisions of such men have been made on the basis of expediency and situational factors rather than on the basis of any long-term life plan" (Slocum, 1965).

The point is that most of the present theories of vocational development and decision-making are based on limited samples of rather privileged persons. Retrospective data has been gained by sampling people at the peak of their career and asking them how they got to their present position and what factors were important to them in this process. They are addressed to the middle class rather than to those who depart from this classification in either direction. They tend to emphasize the continuous, uninterrupted, and progressive aspects of vocational behavior which seem possible in a segment of the population whose limits upon choice are minimal, for whom the resources both psychological and economic are available to facilitate purposeful development, and where a high correspondence between self-concept and career-concept is probable. Such criteria do not fit all the persons about whom guidance practitioners must be concerned. For example, crucial variables in vocational development are more apt to be accidental and economic for those of the lower class than the middle class, for females than for males, for non-Western than for Western workers (Stefflre, 1966).

When one uses such terms as lower or middle or upper social class in a nomothetic sense, there is the constant danger of misapplication. "Unfortunately, lower class culture is fast becoming a new stereotype behind which the individual is not revealed more fully, but instead is lost" (Leacock, 1968). Vocational development theories, while principally attuned to a middle class or a particular learned pattern of behavior found more typically in one segment of the population than in some other, do not suggest or intend that the processes of choice and development among psychologically and economically favored individuals is the only possible model for behavior. Nor do the authors of these theories intend that they be generalized to groups which the postulates do not describe.

Understanding cultural differences, if not confined to the generalized stereotype connoted by some group label, permits counselors to understand the intensity with which particular factors operate, in part because of socially patterned behavior, to restrict or to broaden the vocational behavior and decision-making competency of specific individuals. Cultural concepts are valuable to the degree that they are used to understand the individual rather than as defensive devices which ascribe to the individual some group composite which rationalizes away the possibilities of his positive growth.

There is another point that needs to be raised about the current state of vocational development theory which relates to the ages or the maturity required to make choices. "Most would feel that a certain maturing process must take place before youth (ages 14 to 18)' can sensibly make choices — especially vocational ones" (McDaniel, 1968). McDaniel rebuts this assumption by stating that "youth are not too young to choose, only too poorly prepared to make choices." In one sense there is a parallel between the kind of thinking which indicates categorically that youngsters are too young to choose and the thinking about social classes as having a rigid effect upon every member of a given social class. Both deny the reality of variance and heterogeneity in every unit of the population including the smallest, the individual himself.

This chapter will consider a number of factors, including age and cultural background, which relate to individual vocational development and decision-making but are not as clearly emphasized in the major theorizing about these phenomena as is necessary if the practitioner is to be more than a generalizer.

Culture, Race and Social Class Factors

It is clear that vocational development theory has emphasized the importance of individual factors, and the need for these to be considered within a context of social factors which influence the individual and define his freedom of choice. Probably the most significant social factor affecting vocational development is social class identification. It is within such a rubric that are found important elements which range from family income levels through social expectations and social mobility to psychological support for particular individual educational and occupational motivations. Social class identification also includes integral relationships with race, ethnicity, religion and other elements which influence choice-making or its lack. Lipsett (1962) has indicated that a counselor must understand the influence upon individuals of such social factors as the following:

1. Social class membership — e.g., occupation and income of parents, education of parents, place and type of residence, and ethnic background.

2. Home influences — e.g., parental goals for the individual, influence of siblings, family values and counselee's acceptance of them.

3. School — e.g., scholastic achievement, relationships with peers and faculty, values of the school.

4. Community — "the thing to do in the community," group goals and values, special career opportunities or influences.

5. Pressure Groups — the degree to which an individual or his parents have come under any particular influence that leads him to value one occupation over another.

6. Role Perception — The individual's perception of himself as a leader, follower, isolate, etc.; the degree to which his perception of himself is in accord with the way others perceive him.

It is the interaction and patterning of these factors in the lives of individuals which contribute so significantly to the shaping of aspirations, to behavioral repertoires, and to a commitment to particular vocational modes of behavior.

Stevic and Uhlig (1967), examined the concepts that Appalachian Youth have concerning their probable life work. They found when comparing a group of students native to Appalachia with a group of students who migrated from Appalachia to an Ohio city that: (a) Appalachian youth who stay in the geographic area have a significantly lower aspirational level than do these students who are native to an urban area; (b) Youth who remain native to Appalachia have different personal role models and characteristics for success than those students who have migrated from the Appalachian area; and (c) One of the major problems in raising the occupational aspirations of Appalachian students appears to be lack of information and opportunity rather than lack of ability. This study emphasized the implications which attend a restricted range of role models, limited occupational opportunities, marginal family history, and deficits in the information to which these youth have access as powerful constraints in broadening aspirational levels.

In a similar way, most Negro youth are in lower income families. And, most lower class Negro students identify with lower class Negro adults, thus perpetuating a set of occupational aspirations confined to a narrow range. Many lower class adults whether Negro or Caucasian, unlike those who are more affluent, must be concerned about survival rather than status. They have as a dramatic, immediate reference the satisfaction of basic biological necessities. As Henderson (1967) has observed, this is not to say that these youth can not or do not identify with adults who have been able to model higher occupational aspirations, but rather their opportunity to identify with such models is ordinarily restricted. Indeed, because of the high incidence of broken homes among the lower class Negro population, many youngsters may lack male role models almost totally. However, as Henderson observes further, because of continuing occupational restrictions upon Negroes even when the lower class Negro youngster has an opportunity to identify with middle class Negro adults, he will not be provided as large a range of occupational choices as will a lower class Caucasian youth who is provided opportunities to identify with white, middle class adults. In addition, Gottlieb (1967) found, in a sample of 1327 male adolescents (Caucasian and Negro) who were enrolled in the Job Corps, no support for the proposition that the lower class culture has a built-in set of values that discourage social mobility. Rather, it appeared that lower class parents, while having the desire to have their children succeed, lack the abilities important to facilitate movement into more advantageous social positions and "there are few other adults in their lives who have the ability to help the youngster in both the business of goal clarification and goal attainment." Thus, even though black militants seem not to agree, it seems crucial to Negro youngsters that they have access to individuals, both black and white, who can model occupational alternatives across a broad spectrum.

Role model identification is related to what Zito and Bardon (1968) have called achievement imagery. Their study attempted to determine how Negro adolescents in an urban area perceive the probabilities of success and failure in both school and work. They found that

> (1) Achievement Imagery, or the need to achieve, is equally strong in Negro adolescents from the same urban environment regardless of intelligence and type of school program. (2) School related material tends to threaten Negro adolescents with failure, whereas work-related material arouses fantasies of successful achievement of goals. It appears that the typical school regular and special education programs are not perceived as pleasant by Negro adolescents in the study. However, the future world of work is viewed in more positive, hopeful terms. The subjects in this study, discouraged as they were with their present occupation (school), looked forward to a more optimistic future (work).

Such optimism about work or about one's personal ability to deal with the present and with the future is not a characteristic of all Negro youth nor of youth whom Washington (1964), from her perspective as Principal of Cardozo High School, Washington, D.C. and as the Director of the Cardozo Peace Corps Pilot Project in Urban Teaching, has described as characterized by cultural deprivation. These are the students

> who have been told for so long that they are failures, that they are in-
> ferior, that they have no future ahead of them and that they are just one
> vast group of juvenile delinquents and culturally deprived youths. Many
> of them have come to believe not only that these things are true about
> themselves, but also that there is very little to distinguish oneself from
> another in this group. . . . These youngsters do not know who they are,
> what they can be, or even what they want to be. They are afraid, but
> they do not know of what. They are angry, but they do not know at
> whom. They are rejected, and they do not know why . . . not knowing
> what they want to do, they want and do nothing.

Washington's description of urban students suffering from cultural deprivation finds support in the work of Williams and Byars (1968) who studied the self-esteem of Negro adolescents in Southern communities in which desegregation of public facilities and schools is occurring. Generally, the findings indicated that the Negro students were low in self-confidence, defensive in their self-descriptions, confused concerning their self-identity, and similar in their performance to neurotic and psychotic individuals as measured by the Tennessee Self-Concept Scale. If self-evaluation evolves from the ways in which significant others mirror one's value then it seems that the historical communication to Negroes in overt and covert ways of their inferior status is manifest in the self-concepts of these young people.

Compared to middle-class youth, working class youth are forced by family circumstances to rely more on their own resources to achieve success in school and occupational life (Elder 1968). Such a condition builds an independence which is often antithetical to the social learning demands and goal directedness required by a different but dominant social class. Because lower class youth frequently suffer simultaneously from economic deprivation, educational deprivation, and from racially defined vocational discrimination, their behavioral products result from

> (a) inadequate emotional support; (b) too many social learning de-
> mands without face validity; (c) too few social learning demands — the
> spoiled weaklings; (d) too few social learning demands combined with
> inadequate emotional support; (e) no true sense of community which is
> necessary to teaching moral values; (f) inadequate man's work to apply
> themselves to; and (g) the required use of abstractions such as words
> without a sense of relevant real experience. (Ehrle, 1968)

Many such youth either reject work values and material rewards without any positive substitutes for such outcomes or insist on immediate material reward at no personal cost or effort. They are buffeted by the whims of the moment without either a future orientation or a plan by which the present and the future can be constructively exploited.

To make such analyses of conditions and behavior which characterize youth suffering different types of deprivation is not to ascribe these things to all members of a particular population. Certainly, psychological deprivation and a lack of emotional support are not exclusive properties of lower economic classes; their presence is observed at all points in a social class continuum although with differences in intensity. The point is that there needs to be differential diagnosis of behavioral modalities designed to provide the appropriate mix of experiences which any given individual needs to move in personally meaningful ways. Frequently, a major emphasis is placed upon the need for counseling among the poor, the disadvantaged, the deprived. However, as Calia (1966a) has pointed out "the counseling process, as currently conceived, is highly incongruous with the life style of the poor . . . the introspective and verbal demands of the dyadic encounter, the phenomenon of assumed similarity and the necessity for self-referral, all serve to vitiate the counselor's effectiveness. . . . Utilizing natural therapeutic conditions in the home, school, work, and play provides the counselor with some promising alternatives."

Responding to the assumptions of continuity in vocational development which are implicit if not explicit in current theories, LoCascio's study (1967) examined the presence of discontinuity in vocational development. He described developmental units as continuous, delayed, and impaired with their implications for differences in the adequacies of behavioral repertoires, learning and the incorporation of learning. It appears that the vocational development of those who have been labeled as disadvantaged is more likely to be delayed or impaired than is true of their more favored contemporaries. Studies by Schmieding and Jensen (1968) of American Indian Students and by Asbury (1968) of rural disadvantaged boys, like Stevic and Uhrig's study of Appalachian youth cited previously, support LoCascio's premises.

As has been indicated, social class restrictions do not operate only to the detriment of the poor and the lower class. They also attend the expectations and the demands in the middle or upper classes. In a classic study of the educational plans and preferences of upper-middle class junior high school pupils, Krippner (1965) found that most of them were expected to attend college and that neither pupil dislike of school nor poor achievement deterred these students from agreeing with their parents that higher education should be given high priority among their plans for the future. He stated, "It seems incredible that nine out of ten parents, whose children are the poorest students in their class, should give their sons and daughters the impression that they are to attend college. Many of these boys and girls are working two grades below their present school placement, yet this fact is apparently ignored." Gribbons and Lohnes (1966) found a similar phenomenon operating in their studies in Boston. As a result they reaffirmed the conviction of the Project Talent investigators who said: "We may tentatively conclude that students in the lowest aptitude levels expect more education and think that their parents want them to have more education than is realistically possible or even beneficial to them."

Sex

The differences between males and females are given only cursory attention in theories of vocational development. Yet, it seems obvious, if for no other reason than the biological, that differences will occur in the ways young women and young men approach vocational choices.

The work patterns of young women have undergone notable changes within the last three decades. They seek more schooling, earlier marriages, and more employment than ever before (Surette, 1967). It has been contended by Havighurst (1965) that counseling should be different for girls than it is for boys. That this is a valid premise is supported by the fact that pathways to adulthood for girls are different from those of boys. They have a smaller range of actual choices available to them than do boys. Similar to discrimination which prohibits access to some occupations because of racial criteria, sex-typing operates to restrict occupations open to girls. Yet, a girl gets "set" in a career pattern rather early, generally by the age of 15. For this reason and others, there are more choice points and they come faster than for boys.

Girls tend to "fall" into career pattern with less thought than boys because cultural influences assign to boys a primary role as the breadwinner and thus emphasize the greater importance of vocational choices. The vocational choice and vocational development of males is seen as more critical not because of the benefits to the male himself but because of the potential implications for his future family role. However, since masculine identity questions are more typically wrapped in a vocational fabric than is true for females, girls have a problem of identity achievement which differs from boys. Indeed, the greater combination of career patterns observed in women which results from pursuing simultaneously marriage, child-rearing, and career development compounds identity questions.

Much of contemporary role theory (Parsons and Bales, 1955) maintains that instrumental and expressive roles are learned through a socialization process within the social system of the family. As Risch and Beymer (1967) have observed:

> This process involves eventual identification of a girl or boy with his like-sexed parent. Through the performance of a certain role, an individual acquires need-dispositions and values appropriate to that role . . . differences between the sexes with regard to personality characteristics and values do not occur because of some innate differences between the sexes with regard to these criteria. Instead, sex differences in need-dispositions, expected behaviors, and standards of value are a function of the 'instrumental' or 'expressive' role which is learned through socialization within a social system.

Most mothers are observed by their children in expressive roles which emphasize nurturance, rather than gratification, satisfaction, success, and accomplishment, as is true in instrumental roles. Thus, it can be expected that the incorporation into the female self-concept of her identification with the mother would restrict the vocational modalities she would seek in implementing a vocational choice quite aside from any cultural or occupational discrimination which operates.

In studies which examine the relationships between the vocational choices of girls and their parents' occupational levels (Lee and King, 1964; Hanson, 1965), it is interesting to find that while the mean level of the occupational preferences was higher than the mean level of the parents' actual occupation, parents suggested occupations at a higher level than the girls' occupational preferences and expectancies. The important finding here relates to the incongruity between preferences and expectancies. Like findings among persons vocationally disadvantaged by race or economics, the vocational *preferences* of girls are generally as high as those of males, just as those of the disadvantaged are as high as those of the more favored, but their *expectancies* are not congruent. In other words what they would prefer to do is not what they expect to be able to do. Such inconsistency may stem from a recognition of their inability to do what they prefer because of lack of intellect or aptitude (Osipow and Gold, 1967; Clack, 1968) but the more pertinent reason seems to lie in their recognition of cultural constraints which will prohibit them from access to their preferred choices. Krippner's data (1963) tend to indicate, however, that the process of sexual identification may play an important part in determining the level of the pupil's preferred occupation "even if the boy or girl rejects the specific job held by the same sexed parent." Thus, it is likely that occupational preferences will reflect the family's occupational level and, therefore, the pupil's socioeconomic milieu.

Age of Choice

The theories of vocational development extant suggest that because of the complexity of the factors involved, students are unable to make realistic choices until senior high school or later. This may be true in a great many cases, but Gribbons and Lohnes (1967) have recently shown that it is not true for all. Some important degree of vocational maturity early in the eighth grade is a reality for many of the subjects of their research. The assumption is that such vocational maturity is also present even earlier than the eighth-grade among other students. Vocational maturity cannot be left to happenstance nor is premature early closure of occupational choice desirable. But avoidance of these possibilities requires of counselors assessment of individual status with regard to vocational maturity and of the experiences necessary to such attainment.

As was noted in the previous discussion about the gaps which exist in vocational development theory as it pertains to females, girls do make choices at a relatively earlier age than theories assume. The question of whether these are good or bad choices is not at issue here. Choices are made and their goodness or badness seems to be a function of whether they are made with appropriate input or by happenstance. Current theories seem to be descriptive of what happens when no purposeful intervention to facilitate individual choice-making behavior is introduced by schools, other social institutions, or counselors.

The assumption that students cannot make realistic choices until senior high school or later is coming under scrutiny from various vantage points. In the first place, many young people do not make it to senior high school. They absent themselves from formal schooling before this time. They make choices to enter the labor market, to get married, to join the military or simply to populate the street corners of America, but they do make choices. Accordingly, one can conclude that whether or not the outcomes of these choices are good and whether theories support the efficacy, choice-making does occur at a relatively early age for many young people. Thus, guidance strategies must be able to effect a climate from the elementary school forward which provides opportunities by which the choices, which for some young people must be made at early ages, become informed choices. This need is also echoed by Hoyt (1965) who, as a result of his work with Specialty-Oriented Students, has emphasized the need for counseling for specific decision-making. He asserts, "I think far too many students leave the secondary school today with, at best, some general notions of what they may do but without the slightest idea of how they will convert these general notions into realistic actions."

McDaniels (1968) has cited challenges derived from Super's statement (Super and Overstreet, 1960), that "in grade nine, vocational maturity is not characterizable as goal-attainment, as the having of consistent, realistic preferences, nor as having begun to make a place for oneself in the world of work." Because of the rapid and high level of development, physically and intellectually, of today's youth, McDaniels contends that they could learn to make choices if they were prepared to do so. In addition, while youth are in educational settings longer and in greater numbers than ever before, a large number of their contemporaries are also in work settings. He cites the employment figures for May, 1967, which indicated that at that time more than five million youth from 16 to 19 years of age were in the labor force. These persons made choices.

In addition to the research cited by McDaniels in support of his contentions and that of Gribbons and Lohnes previously noted, there are others of relevance. Helen S. Astin (1967) in a study utilizing data from Project TALENT found that, among a male sample, measured interests and expressed career choice at the *ninth-grade level* were the best predictors of career outcomes at the twelfth-grade level. Flores and Olsen (1967) found that LOA (Level of Occupational Aspiration) is probably formed in eighth-grade males and is possibly one of the first stable and realistic occupational considerations which counselors can bring to a conscious level through exploration of alternatives within a given LOA.

Thompson (1966) in a study designed to examine occupational values of high school students found that freshmen students were very definite in what was important to them in a vocation, and in their sophomore year over three-fourths of the sample still rated the importance of these occupational values as they had a year previously. There were significant differences in the occupational values held by girls and by boys but both groups consistently held at the sophomore year whatever values they had upon entering high school. In a study of the occupational choices of 116 twelve-year-old sixth-graders (Davis, Hagan, and Strouf, 1962) it was found that tentative choices were made by 60% of these students. More mature choices correlated positively with intelligence and the feminine sex and inversely with reading retardation, but not with race or socio-economic environment. Madaus and O'Hara (1967) also found that career patterns for a science or nonscience career are distinguishable by the time a boy is in high school. They found further that once boys are classified by occupational field, they have the same vocational interest patterns regardless of their year in high school. For example, the group of boys electing law in grade 9 do not have significantly different interest patterns from boys choosing law in grade 12. Thus, for some boys consistency of interest is established at least as early as the ninth grade. Such findings are not to deny, as many of the vocational development theorists contend, that there is a discernible direction of change in occupational decision-making with age. In one study of differences in occupational choice between ninth and twelfth-grade boys (Montesano and Geist, 1964), it was found that "older boys use interest less, abilities more, and cite occupational variables to a significantly greater degree than younger boys. Interest is a potent consideration in vocational decision-making of both older boys and younger boys, but the older boys tend to qualify their interests."

Summary

This chapter has attempted to cast the importance of factors such as social class constraints, age, and sex into bolder relief than do many of the theoretical conceptions discussed. The purpose is not to denigrate existing theory but to reinforce the point that what is available is largely descriptive of what occurs if no intervention is applied to facilitate more purposeful vocational development.

While social class, sex and age of students are each givens to which counselors must respond, in themselves they may or may not be of any significance to the development of a particular student. Thus, if school counselors are to facilitate vocational development they can use such factors to create hypotheses about the probable effects of these factors in the lives of individual children. Most importantly, the task of the counselor is to verify with the student the degree to which such hypotheses are appropriate to him and then create strategies by which the individual can overcome those which are negative and capitalize upon those which are positive.

4

Specific Factors in
Vocational Development
and Decision-Making

This chapter can be considered a second part or extension of Chapter III. Like the preceding discussion of specific factors such as social class, age and sex this chapter attempts to cast in bold relief other factors which pervade theory and research pertinent to vocational development and decision-making.

Perhaps the major distinction between the factors discussed in Chapter III and those discussed here is that the former — social class, sex, age — are largely given and constant factors in the lives of the individuals so described while to a larger degree the factors considered in Chapter IV are acquired. Such an attempt at differentiation is somewhat arbitrary and requires some theoretical forcing but for academic purposes it seems appropriate.

For example, the level of intelligence or, more accurately, the range within which intelligent behaviors are manifest is certainly related to genetic inheritance and from that frame of reference is a given. But intelligence, as measured by standardized instruments, can also be raised or modified suggesting that intellectual prowess is also to some degree an acquired behavior; dependent upon the richness and variety of experience to which one has been exposed. Similarly, some aptitudes, e.g., pitch and timbre in music or fine manual dexterity, are highly dependent upon neurophysiological inheritance and are thus relatively unmodifiable. Other aptitudes, like mechanical comprehension, correlate highly with the presence or absence in one's personal history of experiences and opportunities to deal with things mechanical. Thus, mechanical comprehension is more an acquired characteristic than a given and its presence can be increased through exposure to activities designed to develop mechanical comprehension. From a similar viewpoint, occupational values, interests, stereotypes as well as the self-concept are acquired through interaction with persons and things which reinforce or impede certain results in each.

Because counselors are typically more conversant with the factors discussed in this chapter than with the factors discussed in Chapter III, the treatment will be briefer. The intent is to accentuate the significance of the more important implications of these factors for individual behavior.

Aptitudes and Intelligence

It is obvious, although often violated in decision-making, that one's intelligence or one's aptitudes play a significant part in the vocational level one is likely to attain, the training one is likely to be admitted to or succeed in, and the work activities one is able to perform. Intelligence and aptitudes do not relate in the same fashion to each of these possibilities. Intelligence and/or specific aptitudes typically correlate more highly with success in training than with success in work performance — principally, because the latter is based upon a wider range of expectations and criteria than the former. There are also differences between learning to do something and applying one's knowledge in a work setting when one's work skills must be integrated with those of others, performed under tight deadlines, or conditioned by other dimensions eliciting personality manifestations beyond skill performance. "Given intelligence above the minimum required for learning the occupation, be it executive work, teaching, packing, or light assembly work, additional increments of intelligence appear to have no special effect on an individual's success in that occupation" (Super and Crites, 1962). Elton (1967) has demonstrated a relationship between field (engineering) and the career role within that field (researcher, teacher, administrator, salesman, or practitioner) which is related to this point. His data suggest that it is a function of personality which plays a part in the vocational choice of engineering, but it is a function of ability which influences the career role within a specific field. This is also the premise on which Roe's classification of field and level is based (Little, 1967).

The measurement of abilities points to the very individuality of the person by "showing not only that he is different from others, but also that he differs within himself on different traits being 'more' on some and 'less' on others in a pattern unique to himself" (Ghiselli, 1966).

The abilities that an individual has are not isolated from the concepts about himself which shape his behavior and move him to or away from certain choices. They are quite central. This does not suggest that there is always congruence between what one is able to do and what he thinks he can do or will be expected to do. But there is a potential within guidance strategies to bring such a condition to reality for most individuals. Noting that the profile of abilities which describes a person has certain peaks and valleys is not to indicate that this means there is "one right job" or "one right educational outlet" for him which will correspond in an exact way to the individual's traits. Rather most persons have multipotentiality and most opportunities have sufficient latitude to accommodate some range of abilities. Abilities, then, may prescribe the limits within which one may be expected to perform successfully the tasks demanded, but it is doubtful that many choices are based on this factor alone.

Values

As the vocational aspects of guidance have moved away from sole reliance on trait-factor approaches to vocational choice and toward a greater concern with the perceptions and the motivations of the person doing the choosing, the importance of the person's value system has become of major concern. Values have been defined in various ways but with similar emphases. Williamson (1958) suggests that "values are ideas on which people act." Jacob (1957) stated that they are "preferences, criteria or choices of personal or group conduct." Patterson (1959) holds that "values are not needs, interests, nor goals, but values are expressions of needs and they are criteria for the choice of goals." Katz (1963) maintains that "values may be regarded as characteristic outer expressions and culturally influenced manifestations of needs." Values come from within but more importantly they come from interactions with one's social class, family, peer groups, as well as school, church, and other social institutions. Katz persuasively asserts that,

If values are truly the major synthesizing element in decision-making;
if they order, arrange, and unify the student's perceptions of traits and

social forces; if they muster these perceptions for a particular decision or for a mode of choosing — then indeed the student's exploration and examination of values must be of prime concern for guidance. (Katz, 1963)

Goldman (1964) in a discussion of the counselor as appraiser discusses the advantages of beginning counseling by starting with a classification of outcomes important to the counselor. In this sense, he is using outcomes as Katz uses values. He suggests that the model which makes explicit each element in the assessment process would include: "First, the person's own goals or valued outcomes of working; second, the alternative occupations he does or should consider; and third, those of his characteristics which can in some way contribute to an estimate of the chances that he will attain his goals through each of the avenues being considered."

Values, like most of the complexities which stimulate or shape human behavior, are amenable to change. Sometimes the change possibility is small; sometimes it is dramatic in the potential reorientation of a person's goals. Values and their specific importance occur and are changed as a result of experiences to which the individual is exposed. If individual patterns are formed by age ten and tend to persist through adolescence (Peck and Havighurst, 1960); if children "tend to introject values through identification with models," and if "they usually obtain their values from parental models but also from teacher and other significant adult models" (Hutt and Miller, 1949); and, if values determine goals, goals define identity, and if the problem of identity is secondary therefore to some basic trouble about values, (Wheelis, 1958), it follows that guidance strategies, as they relate to vocational development and decision-making, must attend to not only what values individuals hold but what values they can or should develop.

Occupational Prestige, Occupational Stereotype, Interests and Needs

As one relates individual values to goals and to identity, factors of occupational prestige and/or occupational stereotypes are also relevant. Values ascribed to some kinds of work either attract or repel specific individuals. In this sense they act as filters or screens of the degree to which some individuals will explore certain occupations. One study (Ulrich, Hechlik and Roeber, 1966) has suggested that occupational stereotypes may serve as a psychological threshold for occupational explorations and career planning. Consequently, just as the counselor needs to begin with clarification of the individual's value system it is equally likely that the counselee's stereotypes of occupations need to be clarified, since possible alternative lines of choices evolve from such deliberations.

Roe's eight occupational categories previously cited in this text primarily relate to one's orientation to or away from persons and things. Her circular array describing occupational groups which are contiguous to each other but which emphasize people or things has been found to be valid as a description of the occupational preferences of high school students (Jones, 1965). Perrone (1964) found that high school boys with similar scores on cognitive measures tend to indicate a preference for similar occupational groups as defined by Roe's eight occupational fields. Indeed, when job changes are examined it has also been found that such change is non-random. That is, people typically move from a job in one group to another in the same group as defined by Roe's field classifications. They do not move to groups in which the orientation or the activity is in direct opposition to the initial occupational area from which they absent themselves (Hutchinson and Roe, 1968).

On what basis are individual choices of groups made? The answer blends individual interests, occupational prestige, and stereotype. Shartle (1959) contends that the expressed occupational preferences of high school students are largely affected by the prestige or status which they assign to the various occupations of the world of work. These findings are not surprising in view of the fact that the prestige order of occupations is remarkably stable. Hakel, Hollman, and Durnett (1968) found a high consistency of prestige over a range of 42 years. High school students, for the most part, will express vocational preferences for occupations which have a higher status or prestige value than of jobs they will have when they actually become involved on the labor market. Hoppock, too, (1957) has stressed that the desire for wealth, status, or glamor, may lead students to make occupational choices of a fantasy nature. In order to meet his needs, the student may disregard his own qualifications. Slocum and Bowles (1968) in a study of 2835 high school juniors and seniors found that while 68.5 percent reported that they would like to have a career in a professional occupation if they could do whatever they chose, but when asked what they expected to do 43.1 percent named a professional occupation. Indeed, when further questions were asked about the attractiveness of occupations, professional and non-professional, it was found that there was not a direct correspondence with typical prestige ratings of these occupations. These researchers also found that it was not so much that students were unattracted to occupations other than the prestigeful and the professional, but that they did not have available to them information and opportunities to explore the nature of the work and career opportunities in these occupations. Interestingly, in view of popular attitudes about youth disenchantment with business and the dehumanizing characteristics of corporate organizations, both the study by Slocum and Bowles and a study by Lawrie (1968) found a substantial minority of the subjects of their research to be interested in business careers although Lawrie found a negative relation between student quality and intention to enter business careers.

Heath and Strowig (1967) in a follow-up of 2230 male Wisconsin high school graduates found that family background factors and aspiration levels are not as important in predicting occupational status as are further education and training, high school achievement, and community of orientation in a highly industrialized urban technology. Wagman (1968) has found in a study of parental influence on occupational values that (1) there are distinctively patterned differences in the occupational value structure of sons and their parents and of daughters and their parents; (2) these differences reflect existing realistic or stereotyped sex patterning of occupational roles, differences in the experience and responsibility of the two generations, as well as a closer similarity in the value structure of daughters and their mothers than of sons and their fathers and a greater difference between sons and fathers than between sons and mothers; and (3) that permeating all these self and parental perceptions and judgments is an unknown degree of emotionally-based distortion, involving elements of identification, projection, dependency, and autonomy, although these latter emotional conflicts are probably not of a pathological nature. In view of the importance typically ascribed in decision-making to the opportunities available for students to make decisions at home and in school and the degree to which these are influenced by the amount of independence from authority, it is important to note that among ninth grade superior students who prefer to make their own decisions on educational matters, it is also clear that parents, particularly fathers, would rather make the choices than leave them to their children or their mates (Hays and Rothney, 1961).

Needs and vocational interests have been found to have a high relationship (Thorndike, Weiss, and Darvis, 1968). Suziedelis and Steimel (1963) have found a number of significant relationships between specific predominant needs and particular interest patterns. The evidence suggests that specific predominant needs may be more readily implemented in certain occupational areas. Correspondence between needs, vocational interests, and curricular areas was found in a study which showed that personality identifications of students (following Holland's model) were related to their initial vocational choices (Osipow, Ashby and Wall, 1966). This relationship between needs, occupational interests, and personality identifications has also been demonstrated using typologies other than that of Holland. Riesman's (1950) characterization of inner-directed and outer-directed personalities was used by Kassarjian and Kassarjian (1965) to examine the potential relationships between these personality types, occupational interests, and social values. It was found that inner-directed and outer-directed personalities did differ in their occupational interests and that the former scored higher on the theoretical and aesthetic value scales and lower on the economic, social, and political scales than their outer-directed contemporaries. Bohn (1966) has reported similar findings. It is not just a result of typological characteristics that relate to occupational interests or values or achievement *but specific manifestations*. For example, it has been found that undecided students in college are more dependent though equal in achievement to more decided students (Osipow, Wall, and Ashby, 1966). And Hummel and Sprinthall (1965) found that when mental ability and social status variables are held constant, underachievers were less adaptive in ego functioning than achievers.

There are also relationships between educational and vocational interests. In one study, Miller and Thomas (1966) found that an educational interest tended to be subsequently related to several vocational interests, some of which did not directly correspond to the academic area being examined. They explain this latter finding by indicating that a liking for *being* a functioning member of an occupational group does not, of necessity, indicate that the student will like the training or the courses involved in reaching that occupation. The fact that there is a close relationship between some school subjects and some occupations is obvious (Hatch, Parmenter, and Stefflre, 1962). What has yet to be achieved is an understanding of the instrumental relationships available in subjects not directly related to specific occupations, particularly in terms of attitudes and other elements constituting psychological readiness for occupational consideration to which they may contribute.

If educational interests and vocational interests are related either negatively or positively, one can assume that adults other than parents have an influence through identification, support, and encouragement of occupational preferences. Day (1966) found that (1) Some students do choose teachers as vocational models; (2) Teachers also exert influence on the vocational plans of many students whether or not they are a vocational model; (3) Boys are significantly more influenced by teachers than are girls; and (4) Teacher influence was generally proportional to the amount of formal training required for an occupation. That the influence upon student vocational plans, interests, values, preferences, and choices by teachers and counselors is not more persuasive may be partially explained by Watley's findings (1966) that these adults are selective in the students they advise and encourage or otherwise influence toward certain occupations and, one can speculate, toward any occupation.

The Self-Concept

Throughout this text emphasis has been given to the importance of the self-concept both as a dominant construct in theoretical speculation and as a dynamic ingredient shaping individual behavior. Motivation, perseverance, choice, and general behavior each relate to the labels persons apply to the different aspects of the self and to the elements which comprise the contexts or situations with which they do or expect to interact. Self-labels, or self-concepts, represent the pieces making up the composite self-picture, the self-concept system, one uses to trigger or restrain particular modes of behavior under specific contingencies. One's self-concept may be an accurate representation of the self, it may be distorted, or it may be obscure either in general or under specific conditions.

Relating the congruence of self and ideal-self to occupational choices, Anderson and Olsen (1965) found that the number of subjects in their study who showed a tendency to choose occupational goals above their aptitude level and in inappropriate occupational areas was greater than was the number of subjects who choose occupations below their aptitude level. Such tendencies may result from influences in their culture in which a great emphasis has been placed on the prestige and value of occupations that require college training. Or, an equally plausible explanation for this phenomenon is that these persons have not been provided the opportunity or are unable to appraise realistically their aptitudes and their self-perceptions as they relate to available occupational opportunities. The operation of the self-concept relative to occupational choice was examined by Healy (1968) through use of an index labeled "incorporation" (defined as "the similarity between an individual's rating of himself and an occupation on personally significant traits"). His data support the assumption that the greater the similarity of the two elements reflected in "incorporation," the greater the probability that the occupation in which these elements are integrated will be chosen.

O'Hara (1966) has demonstrated that the self-concept relates not only to occupational choice but to high school achievement as well and that these relationships increase from ninth to twelfth grades. Apparently the relationship of self-concept and school adjustment operates not just with regard to achievement but in broader domains also. And these relationships function at least as early as the sixth grade. For example, Williams and Cole (1968) report that measures of self-concept were significantly and positively related to the child's conception of school, social status at school, emotional adjustment, mental ability, reading achievement, and mathematical achievement.

The self-concept, as has been indicated, does not operate in isolation from the settings in which one is located or of the career perceptions toward which one is moving. This relationship has been particularly well established in college students' interaction with the predominant climate of their institutions or their curricula, and it has received a central position in the work of Tiedeman and O'Hara (1963). In studies of the effects of different college environments on career choice it has been found that a student's career choice comes to conform more to dominant or modal career choice in his college environment (A. W. Astin, 1965); changes in career choice are more likely to occur if the initial choice is inappropriate to the student's sex role (J. A. Davis, 1965; Holland and Nichols, 1964a); and that those who change career choices, when compared to those whose career choices remain stable, tend to be more dependent, to show greater creative potential, and to come from more permissive homes (Holland and Nichols, 1964a, 1964b; Osipow, Ashby, and Wall, 1965).

Summary

This chapter like Chapter III has attempted to accentuate the importance of particular factors such as aptitudes and intelligence; values; occupational prestige, occupational stereotypes, interests and needs; and the self-concept — in individual cases and as these combine in interdependent relationships. The principal point for the school counselor is that while any factor can be examined separately, it is only as it is combined with others in the dynamics of human behavior that it is relevant. It is only as the school counselor first conceives of the potential meaning of any factor or any combination of factors that either he or the person he is assisting can clarify its relevance and build from such understandings meaningful plans of action.

5

Facilitation of Vocational Decision-Making and Vocational Development

The first four chapters of this book have examined some of the factors which contribute to or impede decision-making and career development. Such classifications of potential influences upon the lives of individual students are valuable to the degree that they help the counselor become cognizant of the complexity within which choices are made. They are also valuable if they enhance the counselor's ability to be emphatic about the conditions and experiences which cause each of his counselees to be separate persons; persons who require from guidance understanding and assistance which is individually relevant. Thus, the implication is that if a school counselor is to make a difference in facilitating effective decision-making and meaningful career development his strategies must be oriented to where given students are in this quest. For example, it is not enough to provide individual counseling services unless the counseling provided is individualized.

Although there has been an emphasis up to this point on the counselor and the counselee coming together in the one-to-one interview relationship, this is only one of many means by which the objectives of guidance can be implemented within the educational process. Indeed, the complexity and the magnitude of forces which impinge upon individual vocational development lend little credence to the expectation that the school counselor alone can facilitate decision-making and vocational development. It requires of him interaction with the components and the people that make up the outer-limiting and outer-directing elements found in the total environment as these are reflected in such dimensions as curricula content or availability, informational resources, and the attitudes of teachers, parents, and administrators.

This chapter, then, will treat guidance strategies which have implications for work with groups, individual appraisal, or more broadly conceived curricula. It will consider the characteristics of students and strategies applicable to them at different educational levels. Hopefully, it will present a number of ideas upon which school counselors can capitalize and adapt to the needs or possibilities inherent in their local setting.

Guidance Strategies: Some Considerations

School counselor strategies designed to facilitate decision-making and vocational development must emphasize professional behaviors which are both diagnostic and facilitating. To a greater extent than now seems typical, guidance practices must embody better and more comprehensive approaches to the determination of where individual students are in vocational development, in success with learning, and in interest and value formulations. Equally important is the need to make available diverse learning experiences which can be specifically and prescriptively applied to individual needs and capacities.

If one is to diagnose individual needs of any type, one must have a frame of reference about the experiences, knowledge, and understandings which contribute to positive development, which build the ego processes, which enhance a positive perception of self and others, which enable the individual to cope with problems of daily living in a healthful rather than a defensive manner. In the particular case of creating effective vocational behavior, this requires that the school counselor direct his attention to influencing the management of educational environments in ways which maximize the attainment by individual students or groups of students of those requisites which comprise future vocational maturity.

The work of Gribbons and Lohnes (1968) as well as that of Super, Starishevsky, Matlin, and Jordaan (1963) are examples of current and relevant research findings about vocational maturity. And they lend themselves to creating diagnostic profiles of individual status with regard to the acquisition of necessary knowledge and experience at different points of readiness and development.

The first example comes from the longitudinal research of Gribbons and Lohnes (1968). They have examined the concept of Readiness for Vocational Planning which has been cited as a measure of vocational maturity during adolescence. Within this concept, they have isolated eight variables which in combination correlate to a high degree with readiness for vocational planning at the eighth grade and at postsecondary school levels. The variables are as follows:

Variable I. Factors in Curriculum Choice
Variable II. Factors in Occupational Choice
Variable III. Verbalized Strengths and Weaknesses
Variable IV. Accuracy of Self Appraisal
Variable V. Evidence for Self Rating
Variable VI. Interests
Variable VII. Values
Variable VIII. Independence of Choice

The other example is from the work of the Career Pattern Study, a longitudinal study of Career Development directed by Super. The example used here is from the *first* of 5 gross vocational developmental tasks which span early adolescence through adulthood and include respectively: crystallizing a vocational preference, specifying a vocational preference, implementing a vocational preference, stabilizing in a vocation, and consolidating status and advancing in a vocation. Super and his colleagues have indicated that the first of these, crystallizing of a vocational preference, is the process of formulating a generalized vocational goal. It takes place in early and middle adolescence and it is essentially a cognitive process. The attitudes and behaviors associated with the vocational task, crystallizing a vocational preference, include the following (Super, Starishevsky, Matlin & Jordaan, 1963):

1. Awareness of the need to crystallize
2. Use of resources
3. Awareness of factors to consider
4. Awareness of contingencies which may affect goals
5. Differentiation of interests and values
6. Awareness of present-future relationships
7. Formulation of a generalized preference
8. Consistency of preference
9. Possession of information concerning the preferred occupation

10. Planning for the preferred occupation
11. Wisdom of the vocational preference

It is clear in both of these sets of findings that students need a comprehensive body of information which links what they are doing educationally at particular points in time to future options which will be available to them within the context of education as well as within the context of work. Thus, they need to know what curricula will be available to them, what factors distinguish one curriculum from another, what components make up separate curriculum pathways, what personal factors are relevant to success in different curricula, and how the various curricula are linked in an instrumental fashion to different field and level responsibilities in the occupational structure.

Students also need self-knowledge. They need to be able to differentiate personal values and personal interests as these are related to personal strengths and weaknesses in the several manifestations of ability — e.g., verbal, quantitative, performance, scholastic. They need to be able to assess these elements of the self, incorporate their meaning into the self-concept, and relate the relevance of self information to the choices with which they will be confronted.

Transcendent to this necessary base of knowledge is the motivation to use it in purposeful ways. Inherent in the studies of Gribbons and Lohnes (1968) and of Super (1963) and his colleagues is the need for an attitude of planfulness to be generated in students as well as recognition of possible alternative actions, possible outcomes of these actions, and the desirability of the outcomes as defined by personal preferences and values. In this context, students can be helped to assess the sequence of outcomes — proximate, intermediate, ultimate — which lead from immediate choice, the factors which are personally relevant at each of these branch points, the probabilities associated with those factors, and the personal desirability of the outcomes which make up the sequence. The facilitation of planfulness and of career development, then, involves not only knowledge, but opportunities to apply the knowledge to one's personal characteristics. It involves the student's willingness to commit to work a sense of value, ego-involvement, personal endeavor, and achievement-related motives.

Any one of the elements described as necessary to career development and vocational maturity represents a diagnostic construct, the presence or absence of which can and should be assessed with regard to its presence in the lives of individual students. Through counseling and appraisal strategies, school counselors can accomplish such assessments and design with counselees the behavioral goals which for them bring to focus the activities and experiences necessary to move them purposefully from a present level of competence to a higher order developmental plateau.

Guidance strategies related to decision-making and vocational development must be seen not just as an opportunity for the *expression* of certain personal characteristics which make up career development but rather as devoted to *developing* these characteristics. As Gysbers (1969) has observed, "Career exploration programs should not be seen as strictly a mining operation in which only those with certain talents are chosen, but as more of a farming approach in which all individuals are provided with opportunities to grow and to develop." Although this distinction may be subtle, it represents the difference between purposeful, sequential development and development by chance and happenstance.

In counseling *per se,* the counselor can help students first see themselves as some *one* as they give consideration to becoming some *thing.* The counselor in individual relationships with students can help them cast in bold relief the factors and values which are personally relevant in specific decisions. He can assist the person to develop and accept an integrated picture of himself to which can be related the self-relevance of the outer-limiting and outer-directing factors which define or influence the environmental options available. The counselor and counselee can come to understand which of the inner limits of the counselee are unchangeable and which are modifiable. The counselor can assist the counselee to ask the appropriate questions: What precludes my being what I want to be? What is my life likely to be if I succeed in becoming what I choose to be? What immediate plans must I make and what skills must I acquire to move from A to B?

Unless a student knows what personal resources he has to commit or what he will commit to a specific choice and where he is heading, he has no particular guidelines by which he can decide whether any possible option is of value to him. Hence, counselor strategies must be oriented to personal self-definition and to a broader perception by students of the many types and degrees of talent necessary to the world of work. If guidance strategies, and education more broadly conceived, are to develop the requisites of career development, emphasis must be given from the elementary school forward to the identification and facilitation of the positive elements, strengths and talents, which for each individual represent his best coin for future career success.

Guidance and education must reciprocally attend to the fact, and support it in programmatic ways, that students will differ in their approach to career orientations and in their readiness for such thinking. Implicit in such an observation are such realities as the different tempos by which students can proceed through a system of experiences designed to facilitate vocational development, the required translations of information necessary, as well as a step-wise series of purposes or competencies to be achieved at different developmental points. Ideally, if vocational development is to be individualized, each student should be able to work on information or be exposed to experiences different from other students at any given time. Programmed efforts to facilitate career development, whatever form these take, must begin at the student's level of development and proceed on the basis of personal variables defined by experiences, aspirations, values, capacities and a continuously spiraling series of success experiences within the vocational development objectives established.

Counselors, then, ought to have in mind a number of alternatives by which at different educational levels and under different conditions vocational development and decision-making can be facilitated. The following discussion is not intended to be exhaustive of the guidelines or the ways the counselor can influence vocational development through curricular reinforcement, group processes of guidance, simulation, gaming, or work but rather to present some ideas and some activities which individual counselors can build upon and adapt to their own setting so that individual counseling can be complemented (Herr, 1969).

The Elementary School Level

If Luchins' Primacy Affect (1960) is a valid premise — that the information which is obtained first carries the most weight in ultimate decisions — significantly more attention must be concentrated at the elementary school level in terms of attitude development, decision processing, and self awareness as well as awareness of and knowledge about the broad characteristics and expectations of work. Frequently, unrealistic vocational plans are made at this level because of the emphases in parental and community attitudes as well as in textbooks upon "prestige fields," which obscure the existence and the significance of other fields that employ a large proportion of workers. The occupations and careers exhibited should cover the full range of alternatives from unskilled and semi-skilled worker to Ph.D. However, the greatest stress should be placed on those jobs which do not require a four-year college education, but probably involve continuing education beyond high school.

Increasingly rigid walls have been erected between the pre-adolescent, and for that matter the adolescent, and the vocational niches or educational options to which they must relate. In far too many instances, large segments of our student population — those from the culture of poverty and others — have no systematic models to which to relate or psychological support for the quest for behavior which is personally relevant. These conditions occur at a time when attitude formation is in its seed stages. Consequently, the total educational process must support and reinforce those experiences which will generate attitudes and self-acceptance ultimately having a vocational manifestation. Vocational values and attitudes need attention prior to specific skill consideration although current levels of knowledge and procedures now incorporated in such areas as industrial arts could be placed in the elementary school with benefit to individual children. The integration of vocational values, attitudes, and facts, as well as the relationship between academic content and occupations as reflected in curriculum development, is a priority concern. Students must be helped to relate, in an instrumental way, what they are doing in the classroom to the expectations of varying work contexts. Teachers must be made sensitive to the fact that their attitudes toward work of various kinds make a significant impact on the attitudes of students as they develop personal perceptions of aspiration and prestige. It is in these gross ways that the objectives of guidance, career development, and general education must interface and infuse the formative experiences of children.

One example of a comprehensive and systematic approach to the problems just addressed which is designed to help children in inner city schools gain a better orientation to the world of work and of education is The Developmental Career Guidance Project located in Detroit. This project is a team effort in individual pilot schools. Each school has a guidance consultant, a career community aide, and student assistants. Together with the school principal, the project staff directors, and special consultants, team efforts are directed to the following project goals:

1. To reach every student and his parents in the project schools so that they can become aware of the world of work and the many millions of available jobs in education, industry, business, and labor.

2. To work with every student so that he can better understand himself and his potentials.

3. To work with all the parents so that they can better understand their children, encourage their children to dream, and help their children make their dreams come true.

4. To work with community leaders, community resources, and community groups to help the students and their parents in this plan. (Hill and Luckey, 1969)

The activities which are included in this concentrated effort to facilitate vocational development include individual counseling, group counseling, the dissemination of information in individual classes and through all school activities, field trips, speakers, direct work with parent groups, as well as liaison and coordination with community agencies and neighborhood organizations.

More specifically, through the creative use of curricular materials, films, displays, role-playing, dramatizations, gaming and simulation, elementary school children can be introduced to vocational development concepts which are accurate and pertinent to their future development. This is not to suggest that elementary school children be robbed of their fantasies, but rather that their fantasies operate from a base of knowledge instead of overromanticism and stereotype. Almy (1955) states that the six-year-old lives more in a world of reality and less in a world of fantasy. "He can understand a number of relationships in the physical world. . . . He knows his actions have consequences for other people and is more alert to their responses and feelings." Jersild (1951) too, has indicated that children have at an early age greater capacities for learning to meet, understand, and deal effectively with realities than has been assumed in psychological theories or in educational practice. Through the interaction of counselors and teachers sensitive to the requisites of vocational development, identification of those students requiring specific experiences to cope with the developmental tasks demanded of them can be placed in process.

Gross (1967) has suggested that preparation for work life involves four dimensions: (a) preparation for life in an organization, involving authority, security quests, impersonality, routine, conflict, mobility, and demotion; (b) preparation for a set of role relationships; (c) preparation for a level of consumption, involving a certain style of life; and (d) preparation for an occupational career, involving changes in the nature of jobs, and different types of jobs depending on the position in the life cycle. Such topical areas would seem to lend themselves to language arts, social studies, science, geography or, in fact, virtually any elementary school endeavor. Such themes are not confined to the elementary school population but could create organizing concepts which spiral in increasing complexity throughout the educational continuum. Blocher (1966) too, has discussed the importance of social roles as they relate to developing human effectiveness. Students could examine social roles as they relate to leadership, creative or original contributions, helping relationships, and unusual levels of accomplishment. The study of social roles could be extended to occupational fields and levels of responsibilities as well as to such areas as coping behaviors and their implications for growth and development.

Goff (1967) demonstrated in two socio-economically different elementary schools that measurable increments in vocational knowledge, level of occupational aspiration and realism of occupational choice can be attained through a planned vocational-guidance program. Stress was placed upon developing a respect for all levels of human endeavor, toward gaining an understanding of personal strengths and limitations, and toward acquiring satisfaction in the task of learning itself. Children were asked to work through the making of occupational choices for the purpose of testing and discussion as well as to reinforce the idea that early and specific choices were not expected at the elementary school levels.

In an attempt to determine whether primary grade children could gain occupational awareness important to vocational attitude and value formation, Wellington and Olechowski (1966) found that eight-year-old youngsters could: develop a respect for other people, the work they do, and the contributions made by providing production and services for everyone; understand that occupations have advantages and disadvantages for the worker; understand some of the interdependent relationships of workers. The group of students with which Wellington and Olechowski worked was first exposed to a unit of study entitled "Shelter." The building industry and the variety of workers related to the industry were explored. Initial indications were that youngsters at the conclusion of the unit did not yet understand the workers' role and function. Follow-up discussions were then focused on methods for increasing the children's understanding. The students were assigned to interview a variety of workers. With the assistance of the teacher and the counselor, the students developed questions to be asked in the interviews. The interviews and the class discussions which followed were taped. After the children listened to the tapes and completed their discussions concerning the building industry and its workers, there was a significant increase in the students' understanding and awareness of working people and their work. The important point is that the initial lack of increased student awareness was a result of faulty techniques not a lack of student ability to grasp the concept.

Vocational guidance or exploration at the elementary school level and later can not be confined to an informational service although relevant, comprehensive information is vital. Arbuckle (1963) has suggested that the world of work be viewed at the elementary school level as a "world of people" thus emphasizing the importance of individual characteristics in shaping one's future work life and diminishing the remoteness, the outside-the-person focus, which work is perceived frequently as having.

Kaback (1966) has indicated that "the younger the child the greater the interest in the actual job performance itself. Most children are natural born actors; they want to act out in order to understand what it feels like to be a carpenter or a ball player." There are several important implications here. First, in terms of media of vocational exploration, in the elementary school particularly, the use of dramatizations, role-playing, and simulation, each have potential for allowing youngsters to try on possible occupational roles. In one instance, a 25-minute operetta, *When I Grow Up*, was developed for use in grades K–3 to give children an awareness of different work roles and to help in self-concept development (Cook, 1968). Secondly, it is possible to facilitate student identification with attainable vocations represented in their immediate neighborhoods or community. Finally, if children base their occupational preferences on job performance itself, this is a prime time to introduce them to the relationship between interests and occupation areas. An array of experiences can be built upon how interests develop and their importance in life. Interest themes can also be related to change as a process, to capacities, to values, to decision-making or any other process.

A set of materials encompassing these concepts specifically designed for use in grades five, six, and seven were developed by personnel of the Abington School District in Pennsylvania under a grant from the Pennsylvania Department of Public Instruction (Abington School District, 1967–68). The model they developed drew upon the resources of the school, home, and community. As one piece of this model, six sessions were developed in grade five to explore the concept of interests. The sessions were developed so that they could be integrated in the language arts curriculum and contribute to student development in the area of spoken and written communications. The objectives for these sessions were met through:

1. A card game which demonstrated how interests develop.

2. Short stories based upon characters with whom students could readily identify.

3. An interest inventory designed to obtain a profile of the interests of students through media which were relevant to their age level.

4. An "open-ended" play, illustrating the influence of interests on personal relationships, which provided students the opportunity to write a second act showing the outcome of the situation.

5. A taped series of role-played interviews with various workers in which the students were to determine the occupation from the interests described by the person interviewed.

Similar experiences were created in grades six and seven to facilitate awareness of change, values, educational and occupational relationships and similar pertinent concepts as these interacted with student development. In grade six, all the activities developed were geared to the topic,

"Changes that are taking place, decisions which are made, and how they affect our lives." The theme of grade seven was, "Our values — how they influence our decisions and our lives."

In a sense, many of the possibilities for influencing awareness of career development in the elementary school are built upon the premise that at the base of later career differentiation and integration must be a foundation (O'Hara, 1968). And this foundation has as a basic ingredient the development of a language of vocations, a base for personal imagery and symbolization. Through the acquisition of relevant words, children begin to accommodate to cues by which they differentiate and integrate both the world around them and themselves as part of this world.

Junior High School Level

Many of the concepts and methods introduced at the elementary school level can be reshaped and extended to the junior high school level. It must be remembered, however, that as a result of experience and growth, students at this level have needs and abilities which are different from those of either elementary or secondary school pupils. Students of this age level are more able than elementary school pupils to comprehend relationships and to use abstract terms and symbols; they are in a period where they are preoccupied with belonging and conforming while they are also attempting to achieve independence from their families and sort themselves from the mass. They are enmeshed in the continued development, refinement, and strengthening of basic academic skills begun in the elementary school and they are beginning to converge on the more specialized experience of the secondary school. Because particular choices of curricula or of the specific high school they will attend are rapidly approaching, however, their sensitivity to work and its personal relevance to them as creatures who will "become" is accentuated.

The junior high school is a time when intensive — almost frenetic — exploration can be expected. It is also a period when many students will absent themselves from formal education permanently. It is a period when such career development concepts as compromise become operational as realities, and ideals are reality-tested through curricular and extra-curricular experiences. Thus, experiences designed for these students must be timely and immediate to the questions which they are asking themselves. It is a time when student responsibilities through participation in planning can be related to the consequences of decisions made. It is a time when sex differences exert important influences in curriculum choice and when choice considerations become different in kind and value for males and females (Cass and Tiedeman, 1960). It is also a time when because of the unevenness of development, there are wide ranges of maturity within the population and within individuals.

It is inevitable that the junior-high-school student will move toward a conception of self as seen against a background of work. For some youngsters at this level purely academic content holds no appeal at all unless its immediate relevance to salable skills can be made obvious. These students need access to a skill-centered curriculum, to vocational education if you will, at what is organizationally the seventh through ninth grades. If they do not receive this opportunity, the chances are that they will leave the school as unemployable. Some of these young people do not have the tolerance or the ego-strength to wade through a morass of personally meaningless experiences until the ninth, tenth, or eleventh grades when they can get their hands on the tangible and the concrete. This is not to imply that these students should not be provided the experiences which will facilitate vocational development beyond the narrowness of task skills. Indeed, it is within the context of skill development that they can be helped not only to see where they might go but that prescriptions of the specific ways by which they can implement their goals can be created. For those persons for whom skill-centered learning is most relevant and the source of success experiences, training in decision-making and in planning which transcends job layouts can facilitate their self-understanding and their recognition of alternative goals to which they can respond. The concept of continuing to learn throughout one's work life through apprenticeships, on the job-training, post-secondary vocational/technical schools and other experiences can be introduced and explored.

Integral to skill-centered access for some students and different exploratory experiences for students not requiring skill emphases is work itself. Work for many students will be the best of all tryout experiences. For some students, organized work and study programs are ways of shortening the period of economic and psychological dependence under which so many youth chafe. To facilitate vocational development, however, such work experience should be more than casual, unsystematic ventures into whatever chance opportunity presents itself. Rather, the individual behavioral goals to be attained which were cited earlier are pertinent here also. They represent motivational as well as diagnostic possibilities to which work can be related. If such a possibility is to be realized, however, education and industry will need to come together in mutually creative exchanges in order to provide such opportunities systematically. This would seem to require that schools accept a responsibility for placing youth in jobs on a part-time or summer basis where they can make use of what they have learned.

An attempt to use work as a way of accomplishing some of these goals in the junior high school is the Forsyth Program conducted in Forsyth County, Georgia. This is an attempt to reconstruct at grades 7, 8, and 9 the total educational environment in order to render it meaningful to socio-economically disadvantaged students who are indifferent to abstract curricula or who have developed basic attitudes of indifference toward work. The concrete elements of a particular vocational program such as industrial arts, home economics, or agriculture is used as the core around which the basic academic curriculum (Math, Science, and Communication Skills) is centered. Students are placed in work stations either within the school or outside the school, and the experiences obtained by the student within the work setting and those encountered within the school are used as the basis for daily, group counseling sessions. The group counseling sessions are conducted by an Educational and Work Experience Coordinator who also places and supervises students in their work stations and coordinates the activities of those teachers assigned to work with students enrolled in the project (Bottoms and Matheny, 1969).

If work as a try-out experience can not be made available to all junior high school students or if it is not relevant for some individuals, one of the alternatives is the purposeful wedding of educational technology to career development. Until now, educational technology has been more concerned with how to communicate rather than what to communicate. It has, however, clear and powerful potential in simulating career development and decision-making processes, contingencies, and outcomes as well as a medium for translating informational retrieval in terms of individual needs. Many relevant projects already exist. Among them are the following:

1. The work of Loughary, Friesen, and Hurst (1966) in developing Autocon, a computer-based automatic counseling simulation system.

2. The development of a Man-Machine Counseling System (Cogswell, Donahue, Estavan, and Rosenquist, 1966) which among other things will track students through their school progress by computer to identify counseling problems and will automate interviews to help students in the areas of course programming, post high school educational planning and vocational exploration.

3. The computerization of vocational information using Roe's field and level classification and relating student information to this classification for the purpose of conversation between computers and

students about decision-making (Harris, 1968). The Computerized Vocational Information Service (CVIS) at the Willowbrook High School in suburban Chicago employs computer technology for systematizing, retrieving, and applying masses of information to assist students in making better-informed vocational and educational decisions. Data (e.g., achievement records, test results, and interest inventories) regarding each student is stored in the computer ready to be called upon during the retrieval process. Thus, many of the factors which the individual should consider in career exploration are available in the computer and are automatically inserted into the process wherever applicable.

4. Life career games, in which students plan the life of a fictitious student within simulated environments and receive feedback on the possible consequences of their decision (Boocock, 1967).

5. The work of Gellatt and his associates in the Palo Alto public schools, in which locally developed probability data as well as general probability data available from government and commercial sources were used in the group guidance program. A control group which received no probability data was also included. In an evaluative design integral to this project, it was found that the group which received local probability data scored significantly higher on knowledge about the process of decision-making, awareness of high school and college alternatives, and knowledge of the probabilities involved in these alternatives than did the group receiving general probability data or the control group which received no probability data (Yabroff, 1964).

These projects are not intended to supplant teachers or counselors, but it is probable that with increasing sophistication the outcomes of these projects will cause a reordering of the possible uses to which teachers and counselors can put their energies.

To return again to curriculum content *per se*, it is necessary that a body of content be identified which is relevant here. The concept of change as it relates to characteristics of the self and to environmental options has been mentioned as a thread which can complement vocational development and decision-making. In the junior high school such a theme can be related to implications of accelerating application of new technological discoveries to the occupational structure. It can reinforce the validity of preparing oneself to be versatile and yet firmly grounded in the fundamental processes which undergird all occupations. Such a continuing concept can be related to work habits, mechanical principles, electrical principles, structural design and representation, chemical and biological principles, numerical operations and measurement, or verbal communication as this is related to supervisor-subordinate relationships and human relationships. In this context, students can be increasingly encouraged to ask of occupational areas not only do I like it? but What does it take? and Do I have what it takes? In addition to simulated and work experiences, these kinds of questions can be tested in various courses. Students can be encouraged to ask such questions as, Why am I taking chemistry or algebra or English? and How can I use it? And, teachers must be encouraged to respond to these questions as meaningful and as ones for which there are fairly specific answers.

A relevant technique for synthesizing many of these suggestions is that used by Lockwood, Smith, and Trezise (1968). They took the position that if students are even to begin making meaningful vocational investigations, they must first become more aware of the almost infinite possibilities that are open to them — their world must be enlarged. Students were, therefore, introduced to four worlds: the Natural, the Technological, the Aesthetic, and the Human World. In the Natural World, the students studied not only what nature has to offer men both materially and spiritually, they also looked into man's preoccupation with the destruction of nature. In the Technological World, topics dealing with machines, mass production, automation, cybernetics, and computers were used to stimulate students to discuss not only how developing technology will affect jobs of the future, but more broadly, what it will do for man and society as a whole. In the Aesthetic World, students discussed the role of the arts in modern society and the place of the artist, contemporary trends in art, the "Culture Boom," and why the arts must have a vital place in any mature culture. In the Human World, students studied overpopulation, poverty, war and peace, social injustices and the individual in mass society. The important dimension here is that the students discussed career areas related to each world and the inter-relationships among them.

Senior High School Level

The continuation of career development at the senior high school level must as at other levels be predicated upon individual needs, readiness, and motivations. In one sense the principal concern at this level is the intensity of the planning, individual readiness, and goal-directedness which characterizes the individuals to be served. Specific career development activities must take each student from where he is to the creation and the achievement of a set of specific goals. Here, perhaps, more than any other point in the educational continuum, activities must be individually prescribed and they must proceed with logic and system to permit the realization of future motivations, whether these be immediate job acquisition, post-high school technical training, baccalaureate preparation, or a potential future combination of each.

If the architect's dictum that form should follow function is valid, then institutional shapes and organization will need to incorporate more flexibility, interdisciplinary integration, variable time blocks, individualized programming, multi-media approaches, and self-teaching devices than are presently characteristic of most educational systems.

Because of the importance of fundamental cognitive skills — e.g., reading, writing, computing — to vocational development, many students will need renewed efforts to attain these skills through remedial or individualized methodology. But their acquisition can be facilitated by placing them in the context of vocational experiences. One of the exciting possibilities for doing this lies within the cluster concept which blends an interdisciplinary approach to academic learning with a family of skills or career clusters which are broadly applicable to many jobs. ES' 70 program pilot projects are already underway in such places as Quincy, Massachusetts, and in the Richmond Pretechnical Program, San Francisco, to use students' occupational interests as a means of developing their general and academic skills. Lessons are not separated into such courses as physics, mathematics, English or electromechanics; they are interwoven in ways which insure that students have attained skills which are salable but which permit students the opportunity to qualify for advanced training at the junior college level or in other post-secondary educational endeavors (Bushnell and Rubel, 1968). Thus, curricula can be blended in ways which emphasize the acquisition of technological principles and the personal skills which permit one to make use of the technical skills which are acquired. Theoretically at least, one can train a young person to be the finest machinist in town but unless he is given the personal skills and attitudes which permit manifestation of the technical skills, e.g., willingness to be at work at 7:00 a.m., five days per week each week, he is still unemployable.

If career cluster curricula could be developed beginning at the ninth grade, this would not preclude the continuation of specific job training for some students. Not all vocationally oriented students are capable of or desire preparation for the skilled trades or for technical occupations. Specific programs must be developed for the low end as well as the high end of the intellectual continuum whether such preparation is to be a helper, a dishwasher, a waiter, a lawnmower repairman, an industrial landscape gardener or whatever. Indeed, low intellect aside as a rationale, pathways to constructive work must be broadened so that youth are not fitted to programs but programs are fitted to youth. The existing lockstep of certain training durations and specified training experiences must be broken to exploit the growing opportunities in the occupational world to use the talents of individuals characterized by a wide range of capability. The specialty-oriented youngsters (Hoyt, 1968), who are not solely representative of those with limited intelligence, can be provided clusters of job skills in such areas as social and public services, transportation, management, finance, business communication, distribution — areas which are not mechanical or theoretical, if such dichotomies are viable, but are nevertheless tangible, concrete, and important outlets for a range of personal predispositions.

The "zero-reject" concept developed for curriculum planning in the San Mateo Unified School District, San Mateo, California, is one example of the comprehensive planning required by the objectives cited in the preceding paragraph. The zero-reject concept assumes: (1) that the state of the art in education today makes it possible for every student to earn a high school diploma with significant standards and a broad liberal and vocational education; (2) that more individualization of education is possible through a wider variety of known learning strategies, even though much more research is needed in this field; (3) that vocational education and general education are mutually supportive and equally necessary; one does not take precedence over the other; (4) that work in and of itself can be a rewarding element of the full life beyond economic independence, and it is a common denominator of concern for all Americans; (5) that practically speaking there are no unskilled jobs, only unskilled people; (6) that the schools have the responsibility for seeing that students are employable whenever they choose to leave school; (7) that educational goals can be expressed in terms of cognitive, affective, and psychomotor skills, and that each occupation requires a differing mix; (8) that occupations can be grouped by clusters and by levels, and that they form ladders of progression through the various educational levels; and (9) that education is a lifelong process and that the school provides the direction and climate for continued learning (Champion, 1969).

Integral to any of these conceptions of creating vocational experiences and tying them to academic learning in meaningful ways is the opportunity for individual and group problem-solving. These opportunities must span educational levels. Students can be helped to identify and define problems to be solved within the context of current vocational experience and ways can be identified to solve the problems. Students can participate in planning projects which exploit decision-making behavior through which their own interests can surface.

At the senior high school level, the possibility of integrating work experience with schooling is a reality. The age and sex of the student are no longer the contingencies they were at the junior high school level.

Blocks of time can be developed by which students will actually report to jobs instead of school for two or three weeks or perhaps a term at a time. While the economic appeal is obvious, the training and the exploratory potential must be fitted to individual needs. Hence, if a particular student is interested in business or in electronics, a program could be made available by which he can complete his high school work and simultaneously secure the on-the-job training available through part-time employment. For some students, this could be pre-technical training, for others it will be a permanent job, and for still others exploration prior to baccalaureate study. Prototype programs designed to exploit work relationships for students with differing needs as these can be combined in educational settings and in the community are already underway in Santa Barbara, California; Champaign, Illinois; Cranston, Rhode Island; and Kansas City, Missouri (Burchill, 1969).

All of this emphasis in the senior high school on vocational experience, career clusters, and work is not meant to denigrate the continuing vocational development potential of the academic curriculum *per se*. The types of activities integral to curriculum but complemented by simulation devices and processes which have been indicated as possible at earlier educational levels are also important in modified form at the senior high school level. A continuing vocational development theme in courses designed to prepare students for college will serve to diminish the persistent assumption that college is an end in itself. It, too, is an intermediate vocational choice for the vast majority of students who enter college. With such an emphasis, college will be seen less as a way of deferring career thinking and more as one of the alternative ways to achieve particular vocational goals. Indeed, many of the students for whom college is the immediate step following high school will also profit from direct work experience or from access to vocational experience in the school itself in order to heighten the purpose with which college is approached.

Relationships of Career Development and Vocational Education

Vocational education has been called *The Bridge Between Man and His Work* (The General Report of the Advisory Council on Vocational Education, 1968). If a career development theme is to be viable, such an appellation must come to describe the total educational enterprise — not just a segment of it. If any one part or all of education is to deserve this label by bringing to reality in the lives of individual students the complex of experiences necessary to bridge the gap between education and work, more than narrowly defined job training is involved. It is this very specificity of trade or job training which has led to cries of obsolescence in vocational education and unresponsiveness to the dynamics of the occupational structure. As one evidence that these charges have some validity, the first nation-wide study of the postgraduate employment experience of male graduates of trade and industry vocational courses shows that the majority of vocational course graduates do not, for their first job, enter the trade for which they trained in high school nor do many tend to enter the trade in later years (Eninger, 1965). Thus, the intent and the patterning of vocational education as it is manifested in many current programs of education must be reshaped and reconstituted.

Virtually all of the relationships which have been suggested as pertinent between general education and career development, apply with equal force to vocational education. They will not be repeated here. Indeed, if such relationships are incorporated into a reshaping of the many thrusts of vocational education, the lines which presently separate or dichotomize vocational education and "general education" can be made to blur or vanish.

For too long vocational education has been seen as having validity only for a highly restricted sample of the total student population rather than for all students. Operationally, it has been seen as a second class alternative for those with low verbal skills or for those with technician interests. In the process, many of these students and many vocational educators have become defensive about their alleged inferior status, moved further into an isolationist stance, and tied themselves to training experiences rigidly defined by time and content. As a result, many students who desperately need what vocational education and vocational experiences can offer have been blocked from this access. Students have been arbitrarily separated into supposedly homogenous categories of college-bound and non-college-bound, the experiences for each category being seen as mutually exclusive.

The alternative to releasing more of the potential contribution which vocational education has to make to career development lies not in assigning or recruiting more students for a vocational education track, but in making vocational education an equal partner with all other activities which constitute the educational enterprise. This means that vocational education courses must be systematically structured to teach not only skills across families of jobs, but to develop within students the elements of career development which will free them to conceptualize the alternative ways in which these skills can be used to attain the personal competency to capitalize upon skill acquisition. Further, it means that more avenues must be created by which all students can move freely between "academic" and vocational education with the criteria for such movement being individual need, readiness, interest, motivation and the blend of academic and vocational experiences which can meet these criteria. As Moss (1968) has indicated, it is "the relative prevocational value of various patterns of preparation that is of prime educational significance." To aid students in patterning and mixing academic and vocational experiences, counselors will need probability as well as multiple discriminant data which compare the characteristics of the student contemplating a particular blend of experience with the characteristics of those individuals who have completed different sequences of experiences and the career outcomes they have attained. Such a procedure can not be a once and done exercise but rather a complementary and continuing reinforcement of decision-making, value refinement, and personal planning as these occur not only in the selection of pertinent educational experiences but within the experiences themselves.

Summary

This chapter has attempted to encourage the school counselor to think not only of what considerations are appropriate to facili●ting vocational development within the counseling relationship but of the opportunities which lie in group processes of guidance, simulation and gaming, and the various curricula. We are in an era when the school counselor must think not just of being housed in the educational setting but of how he can make his skills and insights integral to the educational process. The needs of individual students and of groups of students for more effective assistance in decision-making and vocational development give guidance practitioners at all educational levels a natural communications bridge with their professional colleagues in the instructional domain.

BIBLIOGRAPHY

Abington School District. *Career Development Activities, Grades V, VI, VIII.* Abington, Pennsylvania: The District, 1967–68.

Advisory Council on Vocational Education. *The Bridge Between Man and his Work, Highlights and Recommendations from the General Report.* Washington, D.C.: U.S. Office of Education, 1968.

Almy, Millie. *Child Development.* New York: Henry Holt, 1955.

American Personnel and Guidance Association. *Statement of Policy for Secondary School Counselors.* Washington, D.C.: The Association, 1964.

Anderson, T. B. & Olson, L. C. "Congruence of Self and Ideal Self and Occupational Choices." *Personnel Guid.* J., Vol. 44, 1965, pp. 171–176.

Arbuckle, D. S. "Occupational Information in the Elementary School." *Voc. Guid. Quart.*, Vol. 12, 1963, pp. 77–84.

Asbury, F. A. "Vocational Development of Rural Disadvantaged Eighth Grade Boys." *Voc. Guid. Quart.*, Vol. 17, 1968, pp. 109–113.

Astin, A. W. "Effect of Different College Environments on the Vocational Choices of High Aptitude Students." *J. Couns. Psychol.*, Vol. 12, 1965, pp. 28–34.

Astin, Helen S. "Career Development During the High School Years." *J. Couns. Psychol.*, Vol. 14, 1967, pp. 94–98.

Blau, P. M., Gustad, J. W., Jessor, R., Parnes, H. S., & Wilcock, R. C., "Occupational Choice: a Conceptual Framework." *Indus. Labor Relations Rev.*, Vol. 9, 1956, pp. 531–43.

Blocher, D. H. *Developmental Counseling.* New York: The Ronald Press, 1966. (a)

Blocher, D. H. "Wanted: a Science of Human Effectiveness." *Personnel Guid. J.*, Vol. 44, 1966, pp. 729–733. (b)

Bohn, M. J., Jr. "Vocational Maturity and Personality." *Voc. Guid. Quart.*, Vol. 15, 1966, pp. 123–126.

Boocock, Sarane S. "The Life Career Game." *Personnel Guid. J.*, Vol. 4 1967, pp. 328–334.

Bordin, E. S., Nachmann, Barbara, & Segal, S. J. "An Articulated Framework for Vocational Development." *J. Couns. Psychol.*, Vol. 10, 1963, pp. 107–116.

Borow, H. "Vocational Development Research: Some Problems of Logical and Experimental Form." *Personnel Guid. J.*, Vol 40, 1961, pp. 21–25.

Bottoms, J. R. & Matheny, K. "Occupational Guidance Counseling, and Job Placement for Junior High and Secondary School Youth." Paper read at National Conference on Exemplary Programs and Projects Section of the Vocational Education Act Amendments of 1968. Atlanta, Georgia, March 1969.

Brayfield, A. H. & Crites, J. O. "Research on Vocational Guidance: Status and Prospect," in H. Borow, ed., *Man in a World at Work*. Boston: Houghton Mifflin, 1964, pp. 310–340.

Brill, A. A. *Psychoanalytic Psychiatry*. London: John Lehman, Ltd, 1948.

Buehler, Charlotte. *Der Menschliche Lebenslau als Psychologiches Problem*. Leipzig, Hirzel, 1933.

Burchill, G. W. "Work-experience Educational Programs for Secondary Youth." Paper read at National Conference on Exemplary Programs and Projects Section of the Vocational Education Act Amendments of 1968. Atlanta, Georgia, March 1969.

Bushnell, D. S. & Rubel, R. G. "A Skill and a Choice." *Amer. Voc. J.*, Vol. 43, 1968, pp. 31–33.

Calia, V. F. "The Culturally Deprived Client — a Re-formulation of the Counselor's Role." *J. Couns. Psychol.*, Vol. 13, 1966, pp. 100–105.　(a)

Calia, V. F. "Vocational Guidance after the Fall." *Personnel Guid. J.*, Vol. 45, 1966, pp. 320–327.　(b)

Caplow, T. *The Sociology of Work*. Minneapolis: Univ. of Minn. Press, 1954.

Carkruff, R. R., Alexik, Mae & Anderson, Susan. "Do We Have a Theory of Vocational Choice?" *Personnel Guid. J.*, Vol 45, 1967, pp. 335–345.

Cass, J. C. & Tiedman, D. V. "Vocational Development and the Election of a High School Curriculum." *Personnel Guid. J.*, Vol. 38, 1960, pp. 538–545.

Champion, G. "New and Improved Career Centered Curriculum Models to Serve College and Non-college Bound Students and Young Workers." Paper read at National Conference on Exemplary Programs and Projects Section of the Vocational Education Act Amendments of 1968. Atlanta, Georgia, March 1969.

Clack, R. J. "Occupational Prestige and Vocational Choice." *Voc. Guid. Quart.*, Vol. 16, 1968, pp. 282–286.

Clarke, R., Gelatt, H. B., & Levine, L. "A Decision-making Paradigm for Local Guidance Research." *Personnel Guid. J.*, Vol. 44, 1965, pp. 40–51.

Cohen, A. Sociological Studies of Occupations as a "Way of Life." *Personnel Guid. J.*, Vol. 43, 1964, pp. 267–272.

Cogswell, J. B., Donahue, C. P., Estavan, D. P., & Rosenquist, B. A. "The Design of a Man-machine Counseling System." Paper read at the Amer. Psychol. Assn., New York, September 1966.

Cook, H. E. "Vocational Guidance Materials: a Survey for Teachers." *Amer. Voc. J.*, Vol. 13, 1968, pp. 25–28.

Costello, T. W. & Zalkind, S. S., eds. *Psychology in Administration, a Research Orientation.* Englewood Cliffs, N.J.: Prentice-Hall, 1963.

Davidson, D., Suppes, P. & Siegel, S. *Decision-making: an Experimental Approach.* Stanford, Calif.: Stanford Univ. Press, 1957.

Davis, J. A. *Undergraduate Career Decisions.* Chicago: Aldine, 1965.

Davis, P. A., Hagan, Nellie & Stouf, Judie. "Occupational Choice of Twelve Year Olds." *Personnel Guid. J.*, Vol. 40, 1962, pp. 628–629.

Day, S. R. "Teacher Influences on the Occupational Preferences of High School Students." *Voc. Guid. Quart.*, Vol. 14, 1966, pp. 215–219.

Dilley, J. S. "Decision-making Ability and Vocational Maturity." *Personnel Guid. J.*, Vol. 44, 1965, pp. 423–427.

Dilley, J. S. "Decision-making: a Dilemma and a Purpose for Counseling." *Personnel Guid. J.*, Vol 45, 1967, pp. 547–551.

Ehrle, R. A. "An Alternative to 'Words' in the Behavior Modification of Disadvantaged Youth." *Voc. Guid. Quart.* Vol. 17, 1968, pp. 41–46.

Elder, G. H., Jr. "Occupational Level, Achievement Motivation, Social Mobility: a Longitudinal Analysis." *J. Couns. Psychol.* Vol. 15, 1968, pp. 1–7.

Elton, C. F. "Male Career Role and Vocational Choice: their Prediction with Personality and Aptitude Variables." *J. Couns. Psychol.* Vol. 14, 1967, pp. 99–105.

Eninger, M. W. "The Process and Product of T & I High School Level Vocational Education in the United States." Pittsburg: American Institutes for Research, Institute for Performance Technology, September 1965.

Erikson, E. H. "Growth and Crises of the Healthy Personality." *Psychol. Issues*, Vol. 1, 1959, pp. 50–100.

Festinger, L. *A Theory of Cognitive Dissonance.* Stanford, Calif: Stanford Univ. Press, 1957.

Field, F. L., Kehas, C. D. & Tiedeman, D. V. "The Self-concept in Career Development: a Construct in Transition." *Personnel Guid. J.*, Vol. 41, 1963, pp. 767–771.

Flores, T. R. & Olsen, L. C. "Stability and Realism of Occupational Aspiration in Eighth and Twelfth Grade Males." *Voc. Guid. Quart.*, Vol. 16, 1967, pp. 104–112.

Galinsky, M. D. & Fast, Irene. "Vocational Choice as a Focus of the Identity Search." *J. Couns. Psychol.*, Vol. 13, 1966, pp. 89–92.

Garbin, A. P. "Occupational Choice and the Multi-dimensional Rankings of Occupations." *Voc. Guid. Quart.*, Vol. 16, 1967, pp. 17–25.

Ghiselli, E. E. *The Validity of Occupational Aptitude Tests.* New York: John Wiley, 1966.

Ginzberg, E., Ginsburg, S. W., Axelrad, S., & Herma, J. L. *Occupational Choice: an Approach to a General Theory.* New York: Columbia Univ. Press, 1951.

Goff, W. H. "Vocational Guidance in Elementary Schools, a Report of Project P.A.C.E." Paper read at Amer. Voc. Assn., Cleveland, Ohio, December 1967.

Goldman, L. *Using Tests in Counseling.* New York: Appleton-Century-Crofts, 1961.

Goldman, L. "The Process of Vocational Assessment." in H. Borow, ed., *Man in a World at Work.* Boston: Houghton Mifflin, 1964, pp. 389–410.

Gottlieb, D. "Poor Youth Do Want to Be Middle Class But It's Not Easy." *Personnel Guid. J.,* Vol. 46, 1967, pp. 116–122.

Gribbons, W. D. & Lohnes, P. R. "A Five-year Study of Students' Educational Aspirations." *Voc. Guid. Quart.,* Vol. 14, 1966, pp. 66–69.

Gribbons, W. D. & Lohnes, P. R. "Seven-year Follow-up Validities of Readiness for Vocational Planning Scales." *Personnel Guid. J.,* Vol. 46, 1967, pp. 22–26.

Gribbons, W. D. & Lohnes, P. R. *Emerging Careers.* New York: Teachers College Press, Columbia University, 1968.

Gross, E. "A Sociological Approach to the Analysis of Preparation for Work Life." *Personnel Guid. J.,* Vol. 45, 1967, pp. 416–423.

Gysbers, N. C. "Elements of a Model for Promoting Career Development in Elementary and Junior High School." Paper read at National Conference on Exemplary Programs and Projects Section of the Vocational Education Act Amendments of 1968. Atlanta, Georgia, March 1969.

Hakel, M. D., Hollman, T. D. & Dunnett, M. D. "Stability and Change in the Social Status of Occupations over 21 and 42 Year Periods." *Personnel Guid. J.,* Vol. 46, 1968, pp. 762–764.

Harris, JoAnn. "The Computerization of Vocational Information." *Voc. Guid. Quart.,* Vol. 17, 1968, pp. 12–20.

Hansen, Lorraine Sundal. "The Art of Planmanship." *Chronicle Guidance Professional Services,* Moravia, N.Y.: Chronicle Guidance Publications, 1964–65.

Hanson, J. T. "Ninth Grade Girls' Vocational Choices and their Parents' Occupational Level." *Voc. Guid. Quart.,* Vol. 13, 1965, pp. 361–364.

Hatch, R. N., Parmenter, M.D. & Stefflre, B. *Planning your Life's Work.* Bloomington, Ill.: McKnight and McKnight, 1962.

Havighurst, R. J. *Human Development and Education.* New York: Longmans, Green, 1953.

Havighurst, R. J. "Youth in Exploration and Man Emergent." in H. Borow, ed. *Man in a World at Work.* Boston: Houghton Mifflin, 1964.

Havighurst, R. J. "Counseling Adolescent Girls in the 1960's." *Voc. Guid. Quart.,* Vol. 13, 1965, pp. 153–160.

Hays, D. G. & Rothney, J. W. M. "Educational Decision-making by Superior Secondary-school Students and their Parents." *Personnel Guid. J.,* Vol. 40, 1961, pp. 26–30.

Healy, C. C. "Relation of Occupational Choice to the Similarity Between Self-ratings and Occupational Ratings." *J. Couns. Psychol.,* Vol. 15, 1968, pp. 317–323.

Heath, B. R. G. & Strowig, R. W. "Predicting Occupational Status for Non-college-bound Males." *Personnel Guid. J.,* Vol. 46, 1967, pp. 144–149.

Henderson, G. "Occupational Aspirations of Poverty-stricken Negro Students." *Voc. Guid. Quart.,* Vol. 14, 1966, pp. 41–45.

Henderson, G. "Role Models for Lower Class Negro Boys." *Personnel Guid. J.,* Vol. 46, 1967, pp. 6–10.

Herr, E. L. "Unifying an Entire System of Education around a Career Development Theme." Paper read at National Conference on Exemplary Programs and Projects Section of the Vocational Education Act Amendments of 1968, Atlanta, Georgia, March 1969.

Herr, E. L. "Guidance and the Vocational Aspects of Education: Some Considerations." *Voc. Guid. Quart.,* Vol. 17, 1969, pp. 178–184.

Herr, E. L. & Cramer, S. H. *Guidance of the College-bound: Problems, Practices and Perspectives.* New York: Appleton-Century-Crofts, 1968.

Hershenson, D. B. "Life-stage Vocational Development System." *J. Couns. Psychol.,* Vol. 15, 1968, pp. 23–30.

Hershenson, D. B. & Roth, R. M. "A Decisional Process Model of Vocational Development." *J. Couns. Psychol.,* Vol. 13, 1966, pp. 368–370.

Hill, G. E. & Luckey, Eleanore B. *Guidance for Children in Elementary Schools.* New York: Appleton-Century-Crofts, 1969.

Hills, J. R. "Decision Theory and College Choice." *Personnel Guid. J.,* Vol. 43, 1964, pp. 17–22.

Hilton, T. J. "Career Decision-making." *J. Couns. Psychol.,* Vol. 9, 1962, pp. 291–298.

Holland, J. L. "A Theory of Vocational Choice." *J. Couns. Psychol.,* Vol. 6, 1959, pp. 35–45.

Holland, J. L. & Nichols, R. C. "Explorations of a Theory of Vocational Choice: III. A Longitudinal Study of Change in Major Field of Study." *Personnel Guid. J.,* Vol. 43, 1964, pp. 235–242. (a)

Holland, J. L. & Nichols, R. C. "The Development and Validation of an Indecision Scale: The Natural History of a Problem in Basic Research." *J. Couns. Psychol.,* Vol. 11, 1964, pp. 27–34. (b)

Holland, J. L. "A Psychological Classification Scheme for Vocations and Major Fields." *J. Couns. Psychol.,* Vol. 13, 1966, pp. 278–288. (a)

Holland, J. L. *The Psychology of Vocational Choice.* Waltham, Mass.: Blaisdell, 1966. (b)

Hoppock, R. *Occupational Information.* New York: McGraw-Hill, 1957.

Hoyt, K. B. "High School Guidance and the Specialty Oriented Student Research Program." *Voc. Guid. Quart.*, Vol. 13, 1965, pp. 229–236.

Hoyt, K. B. "The Specialty Oriented Student Research Program: A Five Year Report." *Voc. Guid. Quart.*, Vol. 16, 1968, pp. 169–176.

Hummel, R. & Sprinthall, N. "Underachievement Related to Interests, Attitudes, and Values." *Personnel Guid. J.*, Vol. 44, 1965, pp. 388–395.

Hutchinson, T. & Roe, Anne. "Studies of Occupational History: Part II. Attractiveness of Occupational Groups of the Roe System." *J. Couns. Psychol.*, Vol. 15, 1968, pp. 107–110.

Hutt, M. L. & Miller, I. R. "Value Interiorization and Democratic Education." *J. Soc. Issues.* Vol. 5, 1949, pp. 31–43.

Ivey, A. E. & Morrill, W. H. "Career Process: A New Concept for Vocational Behavior." *Personnel Guid. J.*, Vol. 46, 1968, pp. 644–649.

Jacob, P. E. *Changing Values in College.* New York: Harper & Row, 1957.

Jersild, A. T. "Self Understanding in Childhood and Adolescence." *Amer. Psychologist*, Vol. 6, 1951, pp. 122–126.

Jones, K. J. "Occupational Preference and Social Orientation." *Personnel Guid. J.*, Vol. 43, 1965, pp. 574–579.

Kaback, Goldie Ruth. "Occupational Information for Groups of Elementary School Children." *Voc. Guid. Quart.*, Vol. 14, 1966, pp. 163–168.

Kassarjian, Waltrud M. & Kassarjian, H. H. "Occupational Interests, Social Values, and Social Character." *J. Couns. Psychol.*, Vol. 12, 1965, pp. 48–54.

Katz, M. *Decisions and Values: A Rationale for Secondary School Guidance.* New York: College Entrance Examination Board, 1963.

Katz, M. "A Model of Guidance for Career Decision-making." *Voc. Guid. Quart.* Vol. 15, 1966, pp. 2–10.

Krippner, S. "Junior High School Students' Vocational Preferences and Their Parents' Occupational Levels." *Personnel Guid. J.*, Vol. 41, 1963, pp. 590–595.

Krippner, S. "The Educational Plans and Preferences of Upper-middle Class Junior High School Pupils. *Voc. Guid. Quart.*, Vol. 13, 1965, pp. 257–260.

Kunze, K. R. "An Industrial Relations View of Vocational Choice." *Voc. Guid. Quart.*, Vol. 16, 1967, pp. 64–67.

Lawrie, J. W. "Attitudes Toward Business as a Function of Student Quality and Career Intentions." *Personnel Guid. J.*, Vol. 46, 1968, pp. 103–108.

Leacock, Eleanor. "The Concept of Culture and Its Significance for School Counselors." *Personnel Guid. J.*, Vol. 48, 1968, pp. 844–85.

Lee, Billie Louise & King, P. R. "Vocational Choices of Ninth Grade Girls and Their Parents' Occupational Levels." *Voc. Guid. Quart.*, Vol. 12, 1964, pp. 163–167.

Lipsett, L. "Social Factors in Vocational Development." *Personnel Guid. J.*, Vol. 40, 1962, pp. 432–437.

Little, J. K. "The Occupations of Non-college Youth." *Amer. Ed. Res. J.,* Vol. 4, 1967, pp. 147–153.

LoCascio, R. "Delayed and Impaired Vocational Development: a Neglected Aspect of Vocational Development Theory." *Personnel Guid. J.,* Vol. 42, 1964, pp. 885–887.

LoCascio, R. "Continuity and Discontinuity in Vocational Development Theory." *Personnel Guid. J.,* Vol. 46, 1967, pp. 32–36.

Lockwood, Ozelma, Smith, D. B. & Trezise, R. "Four Worlds: An Approach to Vocational Guidance." *Personnel Guid. J.,* Vol. 46, 1968, pp. 641–643.

Loughary, J. W., Frieser, D., & Hurst, R. "Autocon: a Computer-based Automatic Simulation System." *Personnel Guid. J.,* Vol. 45, 1966, pp. 6–15.

Luchins, A. S. "Influences of Experiences with Conflicting Information and Reactions to Subsequent Conflicting Information." *J. Soc. Issues,* Vol. 5, 1960, pp. 367–385.

McDaniels, C. Youth: "Too Young to Choose?" *Voc. Guid. Quart.,* Vol. 16, 1968, pp. 242–249.

Madaus, G. & O'Hara, R. P. "Vocational Interest Patterns of High School Boys: A Multivariate Approach." *J. Couns. Psychol.,* Vol. 14, 1967, pp. 106–112.

Masik, L. K. "Career Saliency and its Relation to Certain Needs, Interests and Job Values." *Personnel Guid. J.,* Vol. 45, 1967, pp. 653–658.

Maslow, A. H. *Motivation and Personality.* New York: Harper & Row, 1954.

Miller, A. W., Jr. "Learning Theory and Vocational Decisions." *Personnel Guid. J.,* Vol. 47, 1968, pp. 18–23.

Miller, C. D. & Thomas, D. L. "Relationships Between Educational and Vocational Interests." *Voc. Guid. Quart.,* Vol. 15, 1966, pp. 113–118.

Miller, D. C. & Form, W. H. *Industrial Sociology.* New York: Harper, 1951.

Montesano, N. & Geist, H. "Differences in Occupational Choice Between Ninth and Twelfth Grade Boys." *Personnel Guid. J.,* Vol. 43, 1964, pp. 150–154.

Moss, J. "The Prevocational Effectiveness of Industrial Arts." *Voc. Guid. Quart.,* Vol. 17, 1968, pp. 21–26.

Moynihan, D. P. "Morality of Work and Immorality of Opportunity." *Voc. Guid. Quart.,* Vol. 12, 1964, pp. 229–236.

O'Hara, R. P. "Vocational Self-concepts and High School Achievement." *Voc. Guid. Quart.,* Vol. 15, 1966, pp. 106–112.

O'Hara, R. P. "A Theoretical Foundation for the Use of Occupational Information in Guidance." *Personnel Guid. J.,* Vol. 46, 1968, pp. 636–640.

Osipow, S. H. *Theories of Career Development.* New York: Appleton-Century-Crofts, 1968.

Osipow, S. H., Ashby, J. D. & Wall, H. W. "Personality Types and Vocational Choice: A Test of Holland's Theory." *Personnel Guid. J.,* Vol. 45, 1966, pp. 37–42.

Osipow, S. H., Ashby, J., & Wall, H. W. "A Comparison Between Vocationally Decided and Undecided College Freshmen." *Harvard Studies in Career Development,* No. 39, May, 1965.

Osipow, S. H. & Gold, J. A. "Factors Related to Inconsistent Career Preference." *Personnel Guid. J.,* Vol. 46, 1967, pp. 346–349.

Overs, R. P. "Determinants of Vocational Choice." *Chronicle Guidance Professional Services,* Moravia, N.Y.: Chronicle Guidance Publications, 1964.

Pallone, N. J. & Hosinski, Marion. "Reality-testing a Vocational Choice: Congruence Between Self Ideal, and Occupational Percepts among Student Nurses." *Personnel Guid. J.,* Vol. 45, 1967, pp. 666–670.

Parsons, T. & Bales, R. F. *Family Socialization and Interaction Process.* Glencoe, Illinois: The Free Press, 1955.

Patterson, C. H. *Counseling and Psychotherapy: Theory and Practice.* New York: Harper and Brothers, 1959.

Peck, R. F. & Havighurst, R. J. *The Psychology of Character Development.* New York: John Wiley & Sons, 1960.

Perrone, P. A. "Factors Influencing High School Seniors' Occupational Preference." *Personnel Guid. J.,* Vol. 42, 1964, pp. 976–979.

Pritchard, D. H. "The Occupational Exploration Process: Some Operational Implications." *Personnel Guid. J.,* Vol. 40, 1962, pp. 674–680.

Risch, Constance & Beymer, L. "A Framework for Investigating Career Choice of Women." *Voc. Guid. Quart.,* Vol. 16, 1967, pp. 87–92.

Roe, Anne. "A Psychological Study of Eminent Psychologists and Anthropologists and a Comparison with Biological and Physical Scientists." *Psychol. Monogr.,* Vol. 67, 1953, No. 2 (Whole No. 352)

Roe, Anne. *The Psychology of Occupations.* New York: John Wiley & Sons, 1956.

Roe, Anne, Hubbard, W. D., Hutchinson, T., & Bateman, T. "Studies of Occupational Histories: Part I, Job Changes and the Classification of Occupations." *J. Couns. Psychol.,* Vol. 13, 1966, pp. 387–393.

Reisman, D. *The Lonely Crowd.* New Haven: Yale University Press, 1950.

Samler, J. "Vocational Counseling: a Pattern and a Projection." *Voc. Guid. Quart.,* Vol. 17, 1968, pp. 2–11.

Schmieding, O. A. & Jensen, Shirley F. "American Indian Students: Vocational Development and Vocational Tenacity." *Voc. Guid. Quart.,* Vol. 17, 1968, pp. 120–123.

Shartle, C. L. *Occupational Information.* Englewood Cliffs, N.J.: Prentice-Hall, 1959.

Simons, J. B. "An Existential View of Vocational Development." *Personnel Guid. J.,* Vol. 44, 1966, pp. 604–610.

Slocum, W. L. "Occupational Careers in Organizations: A Sociological Perspective." *Personnel Guid. J.,* Vol. 43, 1965, pp. 858–866.

Slocum, W. L. & Bowles, R. T. "Attractiveness of Occupations to High School Students." *Personnel Guid. J.,* Vol. 46, 1968, pp. 754–761.

Snygg, D. & Combs, A. W. *Individual Behavior.* New York: Harper, 1949.

Stefflre, B. "Vocational Development: Ten Propositions in Search of a Theory." *Personnel Guid. J.,* Vol. 44, 1966, pp. 611–616.

Stevic, R. & Uhlig, G. "Occupational Aspirations of Selected Appalachian Youth." *Personnel Guid. J.,* Vol. 45, 1967, pp. 435–439.

Super, D. E. "Career Patterns as a Basis for Vocational Counseling." *J. Couns. Psychol.,* Vol. 1, 1954, pp. 12–20.

Super, D. E. *The Psychology of Careers.* New York: Harper, 1957.

Super, D. E. "Some Unresolved Issues in Vocational Development Research." *Personnel Guid. J.,* Vol. 40, 1961, pp. 11–14.

Super, D. E. "A Developmental Approach to Vocational Guidance: Recent Theory and Results." *Voc. Guid. Quart.,* Vol. 13, 1964, pp. 1–11. (a)

Super, D. E. "Goal Specificity in the Vocational Counseling of Future College Students." *Personnel Guid. J.,* Vol. 43, 1964, pp. 127–134. (b)

Super, D. E. & Crites, J. O. *Appraising Vocational Fitness.* New York: Harper & Row, 1962.

Super, D. E., Crites, J. O., Hummel, R. C., Moser, H. P., Overstreet, P. L. & Warnath, C. F. *Vocational Development: A Framework for Research.* New York: Bureau of Publications, Teachers College, Columbia University, 1957.

Super, D. E. & Overstreet, Phoebe. *The Vocational Maturity of Ninth Grade Boys.* New York: Bureau of Publications, Teachers College, Columbia University, 1960.

Super, D. E., Starishevsky, R., Matlin, N. & Jordaan, J. P. *Career Development: Self-concept Theory.* New York: College Entrance Examination Board, 1963.

Surette, R. F. "Career Versus Homemaking: Perspective and Proposals." *Voc. Guid. Quat.,* Vol. 16, 1967, pp. 82–86.

Suziedelis, A. & Steimel, R. J. "The Relationship of Need Hierarchies to Inventoried Interests." *Personnel Guid. J.,* Vol. 42, 1963, pp. 393–396.

Thompson, O. E. "Occupational Values of High Students." *Personnel Guid. J.,* Vol. 44, 1966, pp. 850–853.

Thoresen, C. E. & Mehrens, W. A. "Decision Theory and Vocational Counseling: Important Concepts and Questions." *Personnel Guid. J.,* Vol. 46, 1967, pp. 165–172.

Thorndike, R. & Hagen, Elizabeth. *10,000 Careers.* New York: John Wiley & Sons, 1959.

Thorndike, R. M., Weiss, D. J. & Darvis, René V. "Canonical Correlation of Vocational Interests and Vocational Needs." *J. Couns. Psychol.,* Vol. 15, 1968, pp. 101–106.

Tiedeman, D. V. *The Harvard Studies in Career Development in Current Perspective.* Mimeo, December 19, 1958.

Tiedeman, D. V. "Decision and Vocational Development: A Paradigm and its Implications." *Personnel Guid. J.*, Vol. 40, 1961, pp. 15–20.

Tiedeman, D. V. & O'Hara, R. P. *Career Development: Choice and Adjustment.* New York: College Entrance Examination Board, New York, 1963.

Tillinghast, B. S., Jr. "Choice Orientations of Guidance." *Voc. Guid. Quart.* Vol. 13, 1964, pp. 18–20.

Tyler, Leona E. *The Work of the Counselor.* (2nd ed.) New York: Appleton-Century-Crofts, 1961.

Ulrich, Gretchen, Hechlik, J. & Roeber, E. C. "Occupational Stereotypes of High School Students." *Voc. Guid. Quart.*, Vol. 14, 1966, pp. 169–174.

Wagman, M. "Perceived Similarities in Occupational Value Structure." *Voc. Guid. Quart.*, Vol. 16, 1968, pp. 275–281.

Washington, Bennetta B. "Growth and Cultural Conflict: An Approach to the School's Role in Cultural Enrichment." *Voc. Guid. Quart.*, Vol. 12, 1964, pp. 153–158.

Watley, D. J. "Student Decisions Influenced by Counselors and Teachers." *Voc. Guid. Quart.*, Vol. 15, 1966, pp. 36–40.

Wellington, J. A. & Oletchowski, Nan. "Attitudes Toward the World of Work in Elementary School." *Voc. Guid. Quart.*, Vol. 14, 1966, pp. 160–162.

Wheeler, C. L. & Carnes, E. F. "Relationships Among Self-concepts, Ideal-self-concepts, and Stereotypes of Probable and Ideal Vocational Choices." *J. Couns. Psychol.*, Vol. 15, 1968, pp. 530–535.

Wheelis, A. *The Quest for Identity.* New York: W. W. Norton, 1958.

Williams, R. L. & Byars, H. "Negro Self-esteem in a Transitional Society." *Personnel Guid. J.*, Vol. 47, 1968, pp. 120–125.

Williams, R. L. & Cole, S. "Self-concept and School Adjustment." *Personnel Guid. J.*, Vol. 46, 1968, 478–481.

Williamson, E. G. "Value Orientation in Counseling." *Personnel Guid. J.*, Vol. 36, 1958, pp. 520–528.

Yabroff, W. W. An Experiment in Teaching Decision-making. "Research brief 9, 1–6, California State Dept. of Education, Sacramento: The department, 1964.

Zaccaria, J. S. "Developmental tasks: Implications for the Goals of Guidance." *Personnel Guid. J.*, Vol. 44, 1965, 372–375.

Zaccaria, J. S. "Some Aspects of Developmental Guidance Within an Existential Context." *Personnel Guid. J.*, Vol. 47, 1969, pp. 440–445.

Zito, R. J. & Bardon, J. I. "Negro Adolescents' Success and Failure Imagery Concerning Work and School." *Voc. Guid. Quart.*, Vol. 16, 1968, pp. 181–184.

Zytowski, D. G. "Avoidance Behavior in Vocational Motivation." *Personnel Guid. J.*, Vol. 43, 1965, pp. 746–750.

INDEX